You're Behind It!

Target Tactics and the Unit Lead
System for Sporting Clays

You're Behind It!

Target Tactics and the Unit Lead System for Sporting Clays

Peter F. Blakeley

Petal Publishers

For further information, please contact:
pete@peteblakeley.com

Book design by:
Arbor Books, Inc.
www.arborbooks.com

Printed in the United States

You're Behind It!
Peter F. Blakeley

1. Title 2. Author 3. Sports/Shooting/Sporting Clays

Library of Congress Control Number: 2007925972

ISBN 10: 0-9795367-0-7
ISBN 13: 978-0-9795367-0-0

You're Behind It!

Target Tactics and the Unit Lead
System for Sporting Clays

CONTENTS

Acknowledgements ix

Introduction xi

1. The Basics 1

2. Target Line 5

3. You're Behind It! 15

4. "That Looks About Right to Me" 21

5. The "Unit" lead system 27

6. The Clock Face 39

7. Target Types 47

8. Battues 51

9. Chondels 57

10. Taming the Teal 61

11. Rabbits 69

12. Tall towers, Short Answers 73

13. Minis, Midis and Rockets 83

14. Pair in the Air 85

15. Some Examples 95

ACKNOWLEDGEMENTS

Many people, by passing on tit-bits of shooting information and advice, have contributed to this book. These include all the fellow sporting clay shooters, bird hunters and students that I have both coached and interacted with over the last 30 years. Without them, I would not have been able to hone and perfect my coaching techniques, seeking out ways to simplify the complicated process of intercepting a moving target with a shotgun. This book is both the accumulation and informative distillation of those techniques and I have tried (to the best of my ability) to compile this accrued knowledge in such a way that it can be easily understood.

A picture's worth a thousand words, so they say. As a testimony to this, the excellent instructional drawings in this book are reproduced by kind permission of *ClayShootingUSA* (Brunton Business Publications Ltd) and *Clay Shooting* magazine (Blaze Publishing Ltd.)

While it would be impossible to remember all the individuals who have offered helpful comments and suggestions, it would be appropriate for me to mention a few that I consider had the greatest value. I am grateful for the endearing support from my long suffering wife Alison and the technical advice from my former students and friends Bob Webb, from Dallas and James Teal from Denton. Finally, I greatly appreciated the literary advice from my learned lawyer friend, Arthur Patton, from Dallas, Texas. The unselfish input and encouragement from them all deserves special recognition.

INTRODUCTION

I love to shoot. As a gangly 9 year-old kid in the UK, I enjoyed nothing more than to walk the woods and fields with my first shotgun, a Webley and Scott bolt action .410, hoping to get a shot at a rabbit or pigeon. Most of my shooting skills were learned the hard way, by trial and error. Anything that I shot was eaten because cartridges were expensive; necessity demanded that I learned fast. Before I came over to the US, I spent many years managing sporting clay shooting facilities in the UK and my own shooting ground and gun shop in Scotland. Today, with many years of shooting experience under my belt, when I am not coaching, I still like to shoot. Sporting clays, or quail and doves in the Texas panhandle fill me with excitement. I am also extremely passionate about coaching and I often tell my clients that if I were lucky enough to win the Texas Lottery, I would still coach. I mean it. During the time I spend with my clients they receive my undivided attention. Encouraging some youngster to break targets for the first time or at the other end of the spectrum, coaching a master class shooter until he can consistently break long, 50 yard chondel target always instills a feeling of elation in me.

When I first came to the US in 1998 I managed Westside Sporting Grounds in Katy, near Houston. Sporting clays was in its infancy then. When I was at Westside I met two of the founders of the sport in this country, shooting coach Jay Herbert and also the late, great legendary Bob Brister. World Sporting Clay Champion (and fellow Brit.) Mick Howells was also at Westside at that time. The bull-whip was often ankle deep as Bob, Mick and I would swap hunting tales and shooting theories in the Westside Clubhouse in the evenings. Between 1999 and 2004 I was the shooting coach and Sporting Clays manager at one of the premier shooting facilities in the world, the Dallas Gun Club in Lewisville, Texas.

During the years I have been a shooting coach I have done a great deal of research into finding ways of breaking targets and convert this information into a logical formula that *other shooters can understand*. Is research the correct word to use here? I believe so. Several years ago I wrote an instructional shooting book. Over a period of several months, dozens of calculations and experiments involving pieces of string, bits of wood and countless shots on a skeet field, I came up with a formula that is easy to apply to skeet and works very well. My findings were published in a small book; "Skeet Shooting, a New Perspective for the Beginner" I showed the formula to several of the top skeet shooters in the world, among them 32 times all American Robert Paxton from Paxton Arms here in Dallas. By using the method in the book, I found that new clients could break every target on a skeet field very quickly.

So, if I could develop a formula for shooting skeet targets, why not sporting clays? Would it be possible to develop a logical formula to apply to these targets as well? That would obviously be more difficult; after all, compared to a skeet field, not only do we encounter a huge diversity of presentations on a testing sporting course; we also have the added attraction of all the different types of target involved, the minis, midis, rabbits, chandelles, battues etc. For many of us, that's what makes the game so appealing, isn't it? Nevertheless, reading targets is the basic application of trigonometry and ballistic science. Targets are targets and there is a limit to what an automatic target launcher will do. A quartering target, apart from the subtle differences in the background, topography etc. where it is thrown, is still a quartering target. A full crosser is still a full crosser. A battue is still a battue. So if we can apply a logical and systematic approach to reading every target that we are likely to encounter on a testing sporting clay course, our scores should rise.

Shooting coaches in the UK have a saying: - "What's hit is history, what's missed is mystery." For many of us, when we trigger the shot and the target fails to break, it is just that; complete mystery. So at the end of the day after a tournament, we reluctantly hand our mediocre score card in and retreat to the clubhouse. Over a welcome beer perhaps, with our shooting buddies, we kick the day's targets around in our heads until it's time to leave. But on the long drive home, we still don't *really* understand why the long crosser (that everyone missed) needed so much lead. We didn't *really* understand why the dropping chondel was so difficult. Until now. Shooters need specifics. This book was written to give the sporting clay shooter a logical approach to reading every target that's out there and I do mean EVERY target. The information contained in the book is tried and tested. It is the result of over 27 years as a coach on sporting clay techniques. It does work and the best thing about it is, it will take a new shooter to a high level of proficiency very quickly. In this book, there is no residual information on gun fit, mount, swing, and eye dominance. All these subjects are covered in some depth in my book *Successful Shotgunning*.

CHAPTER 1

The Basics

Our ability to use a shotgun successfully can be divided into three distinct areas. These are our mechanical, visual and mental abilities. Good "mechanics" broadly means a combination of three things. We must have a gun that fits our personal physical requirements, we must learn to control it efficiently and it must respond well to our physical capabilities. There are no short cuts with this. A good gun mount must be practiced until it becomes spontaneous and the gun arrives in the correct place in the shoulder pocket every time, no exceptions. Once you can do this, you will experience what I call subconscious tactile assurance that tells you that the gun is in the correct place as the mount is completed. A fraction of an inch difference at the shoulder end will translate into a miss of several feet at the target end.

We must also be able to move the gun accurately on the line of the target. Targets (or birds) don't fly in straight lines and a gun with dynamics that are matched to your physical capabilities will respond better, making it easier to develop the line. The path that we tread in an attempt to find a gun which suits our physical capabilities is never that clearly marked and with new shooters this "what feels right" factor is difficult to identify, until they have acquired several months of "shotgun technique". Eventually, the dynamic qualities and tactile attributes of a particular gun will integrate and feel just right to its user.

Visual ability means how well we have "read" the target. In other words, we need to make a quick, accurate assessment of the targets behavior *in the area where we intend to shoot it.* That's the important part. The aspiring shot gunner has absolutely no control over any airborne target. Once he triggers the shot, it's all over. As I often stress to my students, with shot gunning, your eyes and your shotgun must work as a team to achieve consistent results. In competition situations, visual discipline is a must. We may use our eyes to see but our success with a shotgun depends on our physical response to what we see. Eyesight, the most complex of the sensory systems, must be utilized to its maximum potential if we are to achieve mechanical excellence. There should be a subtle blend of these neurological and physical ingredients, which we call hand-eye coordination. What we are trying to achieve is an *accurate* conversion of visual information into effective physical movement to move the gun into the right place.

Many of us don't do this. Many misses occur because we mis-direct the muzzle. Sometimes, this is because we just don't see what we are supposed to see and even if we do, we don't allow our brain enough time to process this optical information accurately and we "poke and hope" at some of the targets. This is exactly what happens when we rush a target. Think about what happens on the second target of a pair, we shoot the first target late, and then end up chasing the second. In desperation, as we come onto the second target we don't have enough time to establish the correct target/barrel relationship but what happens? We pull the trigger anyway, in the hope that the "golden BB" connects with it. This is exactly what I mean, by "poking and hoping" and we've all been there at some point in our shooting careers.

The top shooters don't do this, they know precisely where each target will be *at the point of interception* and this is the important part. Most instructors will tell a student to watch the target all the way from the trap arm to the point where it hits the ground. I agree with this but I take this a step further with my students. A target is broken because we have made an accurate visual assessment of its behavior *in the area we intend to break it.* The ultimate outcome of the shot depends on how well we have done this. No other reason. As we strive for a different level of performance, this ability to evaluate the target in this area deserves, no, *demands*, what should be a prime consideration. It's what I call precision pointing. What the target does before it reaches this spot and what it does after, is inconsequential. As the shot is triggered, if we have evaluated the variables of speed, angle, trajectory and range accurately the target breaks. If we have left one of these critical components out of the equation, it doesn't, it's that simple. The only difference between a "poke and hope" shot and a precision shot may be a couple of milliseconds, just enough time to allow the ocular stimuli the brain receives to be converted into a more precise physical response to move the intermediary, the shotgun, accurately onto the line of the target. Then, and only then, will the target break.

In a bird hunting situation, it's different. Snow geese, for example, indistinct and nebulous as they slice through the early morning mist over the spread, see the glint on the barrels of the Benelli autoloader and take evasive action. This sudden directional change with the geese must trigger initially a visual response, followed by a physical one to reposition the gun. The mourning dove, riding the thermals of the hot breeze on the Texas panhandle, spots a glimmer of movement and deploys the afterburners, departing at a speed that would make an Exocet envious. Once again the shooters visual response must be correctly processed if we are to make a corresponding physical one to put the barrels in the right place. But then, live quarry can think. The hard part in hunting situations is deciding what a live bird will do and when it decides to do it. In any case, most hunters would be blissfully happy if they hit 50% of what they shot at, don't you think? How many sporting clay shooters would be happy with the same average?

Clay targets are inert, mixtures of pitch and chalk. They don't think. Compared with live quarry, they're predictable. Sure, they can respond to a puff of wind now and then and sometimes frustratingly seem to have a mind of their own but for the most part, it is possible to decipher their variables and beat them.

Target evaluation is high on my list of priorities with a group of students and the development of a personal repertoire of sight pictures is crucial to success on the sporting course. Surprisingly, some students, in some cases experienced students, when they are asked to carefully evaluate a particular target before they take their shot, often never spot these subtle nuances. When I ask them to describe to me what the target is doing often the difference in the visual description that they give me can be considerably different to my interpretation, until I let them shoot the target and point out why they missed. Then the light comes on and they realize it for themselves. In other words, I see things that they don't. The strange thing is though, more often than not, the shooters that take the time to correctly unravel the mysteries of a target's behavior usually either end up in the winners enclosure at the end of the tournament and at top level competition, there's no doubt in my mind that it certainly pays dividends.

So next time you miss a difficult target go through a visual check list. Was your visual interpretation of the targets behavior (in the area you intended to shoot it) *really* clear or *nearly* clear? Nearly clear is a compromise. Your answer should be really clear. With competitive sporting clays, as we strive for a different level of performance, this ability to evaluate the target in the area we intend to intercept it deserves, no, *demands*, what should be a prime consideration. It's what I call precision pointing. What the target does before it reaches this area and what it does after it leaves it, is inconsequential. As the shot is triggered, if we have evaluated the variables of speed, angle, trajectory and range correctly the target breaks. If we have left one of these critical components out of the equation, it doesn't, it's that simple. We break targets by making an accurate conversion of this visual information into a corresponding physical one, to put the muzzles of the gun in the right place as we trigger the shot. More often than not, the only reason we miss is because we fail to get the gun in the right place. That's right, just plain old' pilot error! If we read the target correctly and we move the gun efficiently, the target will break and the correct evaluation makes the all the difference between a point or two at the end of the day. Or to put it bluntly, it makes all the difference between winning and losing.

The third area we must consider is the mental one, which also influences our ability to control stress. Mental pressure during competition causes stress. Stress needs to be controlled if we are to be consistent. Don't fight it. Acknowledge that this is a normal feeling for everyone. I'm a great believer that in most cases, if we get the first two down and we become more confident as we take each shot, both our mental ability and the way we control stress will also improve. I also believe that work on a skeet field is a great tool for improving our mental game. If I had $5 for every time I heard a sporting clay shooter say, "I don't shoot skeet, it's boring" I would be retired by now. Often, if you ask the person who said this how many times they had ran 25 straight at skeet the answer, more often than not would be "never." So how can it be boring?

A little known fact is that the sporting clay legend himself, George Digweed, was a skeet champion for many years before he branched out into sporting. What about Dan Carlisle? Dan is an impressive sporting clay coach but he is also an Olympic skeet champion. Practicing on a skeet field will teach you two very important things, how to read the angles and how to stay mentally focused. The targets on a skeet field, compared with a testing sporting clays course, are not particularly difficult but running 25 straight under the stress of tournament pressure is. Some skeet shooters run an incredible 400 straight, 100 in each gauge. I've seen the top guys do it many times and it takes intense mental focus to achieve this. Top level competitive shotgunning is a repetitive two step process. Step one, focus on what you need to do to successfully break a certain target presentation. Step two, repeat step one.

CHAPTER 2

Target Line

If we can point with a finger then we can point with a shotgun, so identifying the line should be easy, right? In fact, with a new shooter, I always pull a few "introductory" targets and get them to point a finger at them. This finger point is always accurate; but as soon as the same line development is attempted with a shotgun, the gun starts waving about all over the place! Sometimes, with a young shooter, this is the result of under-developed muscular coordination, so, in this case, there is an excuse. But with competitive shotgunning, line development is of paramount importance. Unfortunately for some of us, this is where our troubles begin.

Many shooters take a quick, cursory view of the presentation and then base their set up and stance on this. With competition shotgunning, it's mistake, for two reasons. In the first case, if we read the line wrong and we may as well forget the lead, because a miss is inevitable. Secondly, incorrect stance can result in a corresponding incorrect gun movement as drop a shoulder and run out of swing. A "drop off-line" with the muzzles is the inevitable result. (See diagram 1.)

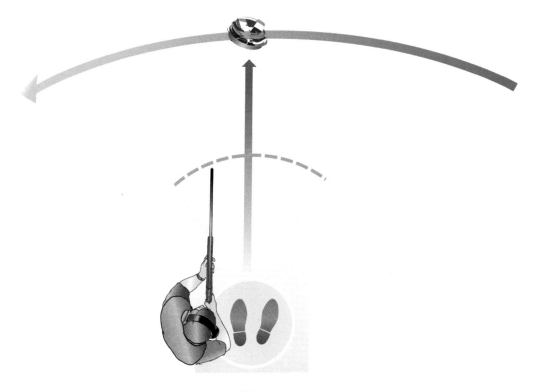

Diagram 1

The toe of the leading leg should always point towards the approximate break zone. By doing this, there will be a 45 degree "arc of fire" to the left and right.

Line is more important than lead. Line is the two-dimensional segment that we perceive the target to be traveling along relative to the position of our eyes. With the exception of the rabbit target and the battue target, all clay targets have similar characteristics. They are all dome shaped and it is this feature that provides the lift as they come off the arm of the manual machine or the throwing plate of an automatic one. As targets come off the trap arm they are spinning rapidly due to the friction between the shoulder of the target and rubber on the throwing arm of the machine. This "Frisbee" like spin gives them stability until they slow down, when they are more susceptible to wind variation.

If the target is coming from a tilted machine it will start to "hook" in or out as the spin decreases, depending on which side the concave side of the target is the wind is coming from. The top shooters are aware of this and can make an allowance for it. All airborne targets, due to the downward gravitational pull, prescribe a parabolic trajectory. The target rises, there is a period of transition and then it begins to fall. As soon as the target reaches the highest point of this parabolic curve, in other words, the transitional segment of its flight path, energy is bleeding off and the target is slowing down as a result. Knowing exactly where rise or fall of the target occurs, or where the sideways drift, as it hooks in or out are critical factors in reading the trajectory correctly.

Without getting too much into the laws of Kinetic energy and aerodynamics, the distance the target travels and also the way in which it behaves as it prescribes on this trajectory is proportional to its weight and its aerodynamic qualities. That's not exactly rocket science and we all knew that didn't we? But hold on a minute. When we consider the specialty targets, reading the line on these may not be as straightforward as many of us think. Because of the diversity of target presentations that we encounter on a sporting clays course, this bleed off of energy may occur quicker in some targets and slower in others. As the weight of the target and aerodynamic qualities vary, so do the trajectories. Simply put, with specialty targets, different kinds have different lines.

A couple of years ago, at a clinic at the Dallas Gun Club with fellow Brit George Digweed I had the opportunity to ask George where, in his opinion, most people missed targets. Georges answer? Luckily for me, George confirmed that most targets were missed "off-line" than any other way. George has won just about everything there is to win in the shooting world and will shoot somewhere between 25,000 and 30,000 top level competition targets annually. Recently in San Antonio, against fierce US opposition, he once again added the World English to his impressive list so who would be foolish enough to argue with him? Subsequent conversations with other top ranked shooters have confirmed the same thing.

Go to any sporting clay tournament, anywhere in the country and I'm willing to bet you will see a group of shooters at each station, capitalizing on the precious moments that they have to evaluate the enemy, by pointing with an outstretched finger at each target. By doing this, they can accurately apply their natural pointing tendency to allow them to identify any variations in the trajectory of an airborne target. With more advanced shooters this has now developed into a pre-shoot routine ritual. With a new student, most shooting coaches will often get he (or she) to do the same. I encourage this. Often, by simply looking at the target, when a student explains to me how he sees the target behave in a specific area, a subtle nuance can emerge after he re-evaluates it with a finger point. Simply put, the visual target assessment is good but in some cases the finger point is better. Some of the top shooters take this a step further than the finger point. For example, have you ever seen shooters standing back from the line of competitors, holding their guns up in front of them horizontally, like a level? The reason they do this is to get a clearer indication of the targets deviation from the horizontal where they intend to shoot it. On a golf course we often see Tiger Woods holding his putter vertically in front of his face to use the perpendicular reference of the putter to read the undulations in the terrain better. It is possible to do the same thing with the vertical sides of a safety cage. By using the upright sides of the cage as a "plumb line" it is possible to get a clearer indication of any vertical deviations the target has.

Am I being too critical with this? Not at all. The gun *must* do what the target is doing. But the amazing thing is, although the majority of students can do this with ease and accurately follow every deviation from the horizontal or vertical that the target makes with their finger point, they don't do the same with their gun. Of course, as I said earlier in the early stages of learning to shoot, this may be due to simple mechanical failure as the student attempts to come to terms with moving a heavy gun about efficiently. This ability to move the gun accurately and efficiently is critical. A heavy competition gun is difficult to start, but it can also be difficult to stop. If the gun is incompatible to the muscular coordination skills of its user, he may "overshoot" the correct target line due simply to the effect of excessive muzzle momentum. As muscular coordination skills improve, the gun should become our ally, our illustrative intermediary. Eventually, the line should be as easy to develop with our gun, as it is by pointing a finger.

All targets are either rising or falling in the place we intend to shoot them. These standard lead targets are either outgoing or incoming and quartering or crossing. If these targets are moving in the same plane, either horizontally or vertically, they fall into the category of a "standard" lead requirement, requiring lead in one plane. So what is a compound lead target? Any target that is transitioning from one plane to another has the ingredients of a compound or multi-plane lead target and these targets require lead on two planes. Examples are looping targets, battues, chandelles and transitioning targets from a "canted" machine and often rabbits as they loose power and start to curl.

All targets have an optimum position to break them on their trajectory. Some coaches call this the "sweet spot". This is where the target is still under power and just before it starts to transition but it is still spinning as it does so which gives it some stability. But target line is deceiving to shooters in many ways and sometimes, establishing the correct path of a target can be made more complex by the trickery of the course designer. Optical illusions are created by changes in terrain, slopes, variables with tree lines and the topography of the ground. A target that is falling in the place we intend to shoot it may actually appear to be level or even rising slightly when viewed against the background of a steeply rising hill sloping the other way. A target that drives down from a high tower against a backdrop of ground rising the opposite way can spell disaster. A target that is thrown at a slight angle along a fence line or hedge at a can also be optically deceiving. (See diagram 2)

Diagram 2

Backgrounds can create optical illusions. Targets thrown at an angle from a high tower against a background of rising terrain or a rising fence line can cause a shooter to misinterpret the correct trajectory.

A simple quartering target my appear to have a predictable trajectory in the early stages but as this same target now bleeds off energy it will begin to peel away from the original trajectory, "hook" to the left or right and also drop. The resourceful target setter, with a tilted machine, can lure a shooter into making an errant move in the direction the target initially prescribes but then, as the shot is triggered, the target can actually be traveling the opposite way, (see diagram 3). This target, although shot later on its trajectory when it is at a greater range may now require *less* perceived lead than it did when it was nearer. With true pairs, visual discipline is a must and each target must be analyzed individually for any slight deviation from the horizontal.

Think of a pair of full crossers, one a standard and one a midi. Indecision about which target to break first, however slight, may result in a split second delay on the second and this target may be transitioning as the shot is triggered. Poor muzzle management creates shooter indecision, ultimately one of the biggest advantages in the target setter's armory. Once the plan for success is in place the same rhythm must be applied to each target, no exceptions, (more about this later.) Choose the wrong target and the transition area on the line will be different. The following pair from the same machine, although both targets have identical trajectories, can have the same effect. Analyzing the target line correctly also influences your set-up and stance and several duck-eggs can appear on your scorecard unless you are careful with this. Developing the line is also dependent on good mechanics. There seems to be a growing trend to shoot with a mounted gun on all sporting clay targets but I always feel that accurate line development is easier on some targets by keeping the gun out of the shoulder and making the move with a combination of arm and body movement. We always take the easiest way to move and as soon as the gun is mounted there will be a tendency to move it horizontally because the human torso pivots easily on a horizontal plane.

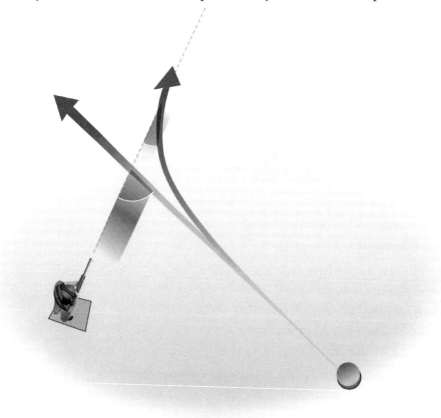

Diagram 3

Line is deceptive. A target that is correctly visually identified as traveling at a certain angle and requiring moderate lead may actually be moving at a reduced angle as the trigger is pulled. The perceived lead will be much less as a result.

If the target is dropping in the place we intend to shoot it, this momentum may be sufficient to drive the gun over the top of the target. Do it the other way and once the gun is in the shoulder pocket movement on a complex line is restricted. I always tell my students to think where the target of more vulnerable to their gun. Usually this is where the target is crossing, not crossing and dropping. *When* you pull the trigger is just as important as *where* you pull the trigger. Variations in target speed can influence where we intend to shoot a particular target and this in turn will influence set-up for the shot. Once again set-up if crucial, good shooters know where they will break a target and reduce their gun movement accordingly. Knowing precisely what the target is doing and more importantly when it is doing it is the key here; this is directly proportional to the range at which we intend to take the target. Most of us flatter ourselves as to where exactly this is on the line, set up accordingly and then attempt to take the target later on its trajectory, resulting in a panic chase after the target, too much momentum in the gun because of this and then the inevitable miss over the top on a transitioning target. Unfortunately, watching the shooter who enters the safety cage ahead of you may not help much with this. Personal rhythm is the key to success and two shooters may each select a different area to break the same target.

Line development at extended range is a problem for many shooters and it is often the difference between applying simple lead and complex lead. Think about a simple target presentation, for example, a full crossing shot at about 20 yards. To develop the line correctly, the gun must be moving on this line and more or less parallel to the ground. Simple. If the same target is now shot later on it's flight line, the leads now has two dimensions we must now not only give it forward lead but downward lead as the target falls. Simple again, or is it? This additional dimension is directly proportional to the distance to the target because the shot charge is progressively slowing down.

A standard, 1,200 feet per second shell will travel approx 0.06 second to travel 20 yards, 0.096 seconds to travel 30 yards and 0.139 seconds to travel 40 yards. At 40 yards the shot column will have a remaining velocity of only 660 ft per second. If we attempt to take the same the 20-yard crossing shot at the additional range of 40 yards its trajectory may still appear to be *visually* flat as the shot is triggered. But as the shot column eventually reaches the target, it will be well into its transitional phase and succumbing to the gravitational pull. Our shot column will pass harmlessly over the top. When attempting to develop any target line, we need to develop an awareness of what the target will be doing as the shot column reaches it, not what it's doing as we trigger the shot and this in turn is necessary to develop an awareness of the range involved, that in turn influences choke selection.

The best way to see this transition from a rising target to a falling one is by standing behind a target that is going straight away, low 7 on a skeet field is ideal. If you pull a target from #7 you will see that it starts to "level out" just as it passes over the center stake at about 20 yards. If we shoot the target quickly, before the center stake we need to "block it out" because it is still rising. Shoot the same target a split-second later with the same sight picture and we will miss. Why? Because the recommended set up for a sporting clay shotgun is 60% above the horizontal, 40% below it.

Unless we are *visually* aware that the target is now bleeding off energy and dropping in the area where we intend to shoot it, in other words if we shoot directly *at* the target, most of this pattern will pass harmlessly over the top. To hit this same target now we must "float" it slightly above the rib. This visual identification of exactly *where* the target starts to transition is important and this is where many shooters make a mistake. Visually, the target may still have a reasonably flat trajectory but due to the delay caused with "shooters time" as they trigger the shot, the target is dropping and their pattern passes over the top. Once again, this is why a conscious evaluation of range of the target in the area we intend to a shoot it is important.

At extended range the amount we must shoot underneath is exaggerated and shooters routinely miss more than their share of dropping targets, for exactly the same reason that everybody misses long crossers; the "exponential effect." The main reason, is difference in the time lapse between triggering the shot and the pattern reaching the target.

We have already established that it takes approximately (using a shell with initial velocity of approximately 1,200 feet per second) approximately three times longer for the shot charge to reach a 40 yard target than it does a 20 yard target. But with transitioning and dropping targets we have an additional consideration. The actual pellets in the shot-string are also dropping as they lose velocity; by as much as a foot or more at 40 yards and almost 2 feet at 60 yards! So, just as long crossing shots defeat most shooters, dropping targets can present the similar problems. At extended ranges we just don't believe how far underneath we must shoot to score a hit, until we familiarize ourselves with what this visually looks like to us at the end of the gun. Exactly the same ballistic principles of this delay with the shot charge reaching the target applies to transitioning targets and here is a method should help you to hit more of them.

I had already developed a formula for shooting the required leads on a skeet field but now I needed another way to show clients how to apply vertical leads to dropping targets. If we look at a high one target on a skeet field, the target starts to transition about 15 yards or so after it appears out of the trap-house window. I shot this target a few times to think about what I saw. To me, it looked as though I needed to float the target slightly, just above the bead. My "personal visual interpretation" was that I needed to shoot about 6 inches below the target to break it and slightly more than this if I shot it late, just past the center stake. I then applied this logic to the same target at different ranges and found that this is what works for most people.

If the target is visually *just starting to transition* in the area you intend to shoot it and this area relative to your shooting position is 20 yards away, shoot what you perceive is about 6 inches to a foot underneath it. If it is 30 yards away, increase this to about 2 feet underneath, at 40 yards the amount is about 3 feet underneath, 50 yards about 4 feet underneath.

So how do you know what 3 feet underneath a 40 yard target looks like at the end of your gun? I often use a white painted piece of 2 x 4 placed on the ground as a visual aid for evaluating perceived lead and angles to my students. In exactly the same way you can do the same with a set of vertical stakes. This is how to do it. Place a marker (a clay target will do) on the ground and then either measure or pace off 20 yards from this marker. Knock a stake in the ground and leave approximately 1 foot protruding above the ground. Knock a second stake in the ground at a 30 yard point, leaving two feet protruding above the ground. Then pace off another 10 yards from this stake, knock another one in leaving three feet above ground.

The distance between the marker and the last stake will be 40 yards. If you now stand next to the marker and mount your gun at the base of first stake, this will give you an indication at the muzzles of your gun of how much you must shoot underneath a target in transition at about 20 yards. The other two stakes (2 foot and 3 foot) will give you a visual indication of the vertical lead requirement on a transitioning target at 30 and 40 yards respectively. I have found that for *most* shooters, 3 feet at 40 yards translates into 1 inch at the muzzles. With any standard or midi target that comes off the machine at a reasonably flat angle to the horizontal, this method works well and these vertical stakes do offer a good visual way to help with the vertical leads but also with evaluating range.

Now I'm sure there are lots of mathematicians out there that are doing rapid calculations on the exact amount we must shoot underneath a dropping target. In fact, over the years I have received letters and e mails from several shooters who have done the calculations on exactly this. These calculations may be important initially, to give us some mental awareness of where our shot pattern needs to go. For example, we must understand that the Laws of Physics dictate that in order for us to intercept a 40 mph full crossing target at 30 yards, we need to shoot approximately 5-6 feet in front of it. Often, this information surprises many shooters. However, in real shooting situations in the field, a *visual indication* is what they must rely on as they trigger the shot.

Exactly the same thing is true of transitioning and accelerating dropping targets. For example, inexperienced shooters are always surprised when they realize just how far they must shoot under a 50 yard dropping teal. Simply put, only the guy that pulls the trigger knows when the picture *looks right to him* and this exercise using the stakes can help with this.

CHAPTER 3

You're Behind It!

Now I'm not a gambling man but I think it would be safe bet to assume that the title of this chapter has just got to be the most popular piece of advice that we hear dished out more than any other on a sporting clays course, isn't it? In a competitive environment, successful shotgunning is precision pointing at its best. Most shot gunners, at some stage of their game, have difficulty with first calculating and then implementing the correct amount of forward allowance they need. But it isn't as difficult as you think. Reading targets is the application of basic trigonometry and ballistic science and there *is* a logical way to read every target out there. So I would like to dedicate this chapter and also the next one, to the subject of forward allowance. Why, especially in a competitive environment learning the correct amount is an intuitive learning process, not instinct.

We've all heard the fascinating tales about Ol' Hot-Shot Harry down at the gun-club, who can stroke doves out of the sky with a flourish and has never had a lesson in his life. Yeah, what a fabulous shot, he is a natural, if ever I saw one! But hold on a minute. All this *usually* means is that many years ago, when Ol' Hot Shot was a tall, gangly, strongly right eye dominant 16 year old kid, he "lucked out" and just happened to pick up a gun one day that was a reasonable fit. The first time he went out, (perhaps under the tutelage of Dad, who was an experienced dove shot); he managed to hit a few doves with it. Then he went dove-hunting every season since then and now he's nearly sixty. But each season, (even though Harry didn't know it at the time), he was practicing, especially when it came to applying the correct amount of lead. Every successful shot he made loaded more data into his personal computer.

He learned that the dove coming in at a narrow angle to him needed a small amount of forward allowance and that the dove flying adjacent to him needed considerably more. Today, out on his lease in West Texas, as the grey speedsters cruise the hot thermals on a September evening, it's rare for a dove to get past him. And it's nothing to do with good reactions. It's nothing to do with perfect eyesight. Sure, those things will help us, especially in a competitive environment but have you ever noticed that in the field, the older, more experienced guys like Harry are often the best shots? Trust me, I know some fabulous dove and quail shots that can regularly outshoot guys half their age. It's almost as though they can think like the birds. But are they really "naturals" or is the improvement they make each season the result of an intuitive learning process?

Now this may surprise you. I don't believe that in competitive shot gunning, there is any such thing as a "natural" shot. Sure, some of us may have more ability than others, just as some of us can run faster, jump higher or throw stones more accurately than others. But then we need to harness this natural ability, nurture it and hone it to peak perfection. I believe that we get better in competition because if we have a strong desire to be successful and we practice. And depending on how much we "want it", influences how much we practice.

Still don't believe me? Well think about this. George Digweed is probably the best shot the world has ever known. George grew up shooting rabbits and pigeons as a kid. Then he was a skeet champion before he branched out into sporting clays. Nowadays, he will shoot somewhere in the region of 25,000-30,000 targets every year in major competition. Dan Carlisle, one of the top coaches in the US at the present time, was also an Olympic skeet champion and shot on the US army shooting team for many years. Olympian Richard Faulds, world sporting clay champion Mick Howells, Jon Kruger, Scott Robertson, Bobby Fowler and many, many more, although they all possess good hand-eye co-ordination, worked long and hard to get to the top of the tree by putting thousands of rounds through their shotguns until they knew precisely where they needed to place their shot column.

Of course a certain amount of natural ability is necessary but to get to the highest level, the top guys must be dedicated and determined enough to succeed. In order for them to succeed, they must be prepared to shoot thousands of targets I do mean thousands, in many cases many tens of thousands. But if we think about it, once these top guys get to the stage where they can evaluate any target that's out there, the battles over. No course designer can throw them a target that they can't connect with.

Over the years that I have been coaching, I have been in a privileged position. I have had the opportunity to talk to, shoot with and also observe many of these top guys in action. They all have one thing in common; they *practice*. They have to. There is always an up-and-coming shooter waiting in the shadows to step into their shoes if they don't stay on top of their game. Many of them prefer to practice in private. But make no mistake; they do spend a huge amount of time practicing, especially if they have a problem target. Sometimes, a 1,000 targets may be shot in a four hour practice session, often at the same target. It's the only way they can get "grooved in" until they feel confident with a particular shot. But that gets ridiculously expensive, doesn't it, how many of us can afford to do that? Most of us can't and even if we could, the time we would need to spend practicing would be substantial. A regular day job would be out of the question. Unless we have a sponsor. It hardly seems fair, does it? A shooter shows some promise and then along comes a sponsor with bottomless pockets and a limitless supply of targets and ammo that in turn, makes sure that his protégé gets even better.

Many of these top guys themselves will take lessons, also often in private, a fact that may surprise some of you. With some of the top guys, these lessons with their coach can be clandestine affairs. For some reason, (I have never fully understood this,) with shotgunning, many shooters develop some sort of psychosis when it comes to taking instruction. In golf, Tiger Woods has a coach doesn't he? I can assure you, the top shooters do take shooting lessons and the reason for this is simple. At the moment, there are dozens of instructional videos and books that will tell you how to improve your shooting. This book, for example is the only book out there at the present time that will show you a *logical* way to read targets. By reading it and inwardly digesting all this and other educational material, there is absolutely no doubt in my mind that you will break more targets. But the problem is, as you trigger the shot, none of this information will tell you where you actually *miss*.

If we get back to the title of this chapter for a moment, it's a scenario that we're all familiar with, isn't it? A shooter enters the cage to take his turn. The target is a long crosser and, as he misses it with his first shot, one of the bystanders instantly, boldly steps forward to give him some "helpful" advice. Sometimes, if the shooter who gives the advice can *really* see the shot string as it leaves the gun of the guy that just fired the shot, this is good advice. The shooter on the station then makes the necessary adjustment, extends his lead and the target is broken. Problem solved. But unfortunately, more often than not, this "advice" is offered by a shooter who is standing some distance from the guy who pulled the trigger and he has absolutely no clue where the shot pattern went. In other words, he's guessing. But he volunteers the information anyway because he knows that most of the time, that's exactly where our misdirected muzzle is putting the pattern…behind the target. Although they may mean well, I call these guys "Woodpeckers." The last thing any of us wants when we're in the safety cage and attempting to stay mentally focused on the job in hand, is someone "pecking away" at our eardrums, quickly undermining any confidence and game plan we may have had in the first place.

Very few shooters have the ability to see their *own* shot-string as the shot is triggered…but I do know some who can. So when a shooter misses, it is rare for him to know exactly where his shot-string went relative to the target. A good coach can see a miss behind in two ways. First of all he should be standing directly behind the student so that he can see down the barrels as the shot is triggered. This allows the coach to adjust the student's bird/ barrel relationship to one *that he knows from experience*, to be the correct one. The second way is he can see the shot string. For the advanced, competitive shooter, these two things are the main advantages of hiring a coach. This ability to "see the shot" or alternatively, see the correct bird/barrel relationship as he peers down the students gun, are very necessary arrows in the professional coach's quiver. Why? Because if his coach can't see either as his student triggers the shot, how can he tell him where he missed? Learning to see the shot-string on some of the shots is fairly easy. Seeing it on every shot, especially with a difficult background, certainly isn't.

I was blessed with an inquisitive and experimental mind and most of my shooting skills were learned the hard way, just like Harry's, by trial and error. Years ago, after attending a tournament, if any particular target defeated me I would try to replicate the presentation on my shooting ground in Scotland. Why, if could break a target in one place and then shift my shooting position to a slightly different angle, did I then need more (or less) lead to break the target again? I soon realized that there were three variables that influenced the lead requirement; angle, range and speed. I would systematically apply these until I was successful, then practice the particular presentation until I became confident and I could break it consistently. Then that particular presentation was loaded onto my hard drive.

As I mentioned earlier, between 1999 and 2004 I was the resident shooting coach and sporting clays manager at one of the premier shooting facilities in the world, the Dallas Gun Club in Lewisville, Texas. At that time, I already been shooting sporting clays for over thirty years and I had spent at least twenty of those years coaching. Members at this prestigious facility would often ask me to demonstrate shots. It's a bit like the "Fastest Gun in the West" syndrome isn't it? Everyone wants to see if he can "beat the coach" or at least see if he really can break the targets. So I would shoot some of the presentations. If I was successful the members would waste no time in telling me why.

"Oh, yeah! But *you* set that target!" they would say "You already *know* how much lead it needs." So sometimes, I would change my shooting position, re-evaluate the target and shoot it again. They were open-mouthed if I was successful and once again, the target was crushed. I would then politely explain that, because I had shot sporting clays for many years, I had developed the ability to "read" the targets and I knew more precisely how much lead to give them. Of course I'm no George Digweed and I didn't hit them all, most of us don't, do we? But even on the very difficult targets, it would usually only take me perhaps two or three shots until I became "grooved in" and I could break them. Consistently. In other words, once I had "found" the target, I would take a "mental picture". It was then easy to repeat the shot. While we're on the subject of George Digweed, when I was at Dallas I did a clinic with him. George showed us all how he could break the targets coming off the formidable high tower there… at a range that was close to 100 yards. Impossible? Nope, I'm afraid not, and thirty people saw him do it. George specializes in doing similar demonstrations at various locations here in the US. When I asked George how much lead he saw on the target, he simply shrugged his shoulders. He knew, but he couldn't convert this into a logical explanation for me so that I could do the same.

Many coaches avoid discussing the process of applying lead as if it is borderline taboo, a magical quality that results from meditation or burning candles. Why? Because they just don't fully understand what's involved. Sure, just like George Digweed with the 100 yard crossers, if they are competent shots, *they* may know when they need to pull the trigger to break the target just like George did, because over the time they have been shooting they have established their repertoire of pre-determined sight pictures. But sometimes, that's as far as it goes. In other words, a coach may know what he sees but then fail miserably when he tries to get this information across to the student *in a way that he or she understands.*

"Trust your instincts and pull the trigger when the picture looks right to you" some of them will tell you. Great advice, I agree but only when you know "when the picture looks right". "One mans three feet is another mans six" they will say. Now, I have never fully understood this, so I asked several competent shots how much lead they saw on certain targets and guess what? Their answers, on the same target, were remarkably similar. For example, if you ask 10 experienced skeet shooters how much lead they think they need on a #4 shot, they will all say the same; "about four feet." Some coaches will tell you "It is hopeless to try to calculate lead," and then go into lengthy details about why, on a long fifty yard full crosser off a high tower, you need to "lead it by a truck length." Well, maybe I'm mistaken but isn't *that* a form of calculation? During the years I have been a shooting coach I have done a great deal of research into finding ways to calculate forward allowance and then convert this information into a logical formula that *other shooters can understand.* Is research the correct word to use here? I believe so.

Our ability to judge distance, angle and speed of external objects is something we do all the time with other sports that rely on hand-eye coordination, so why should shot gunning be any different? It isn't. Shooting makes no greater demand on our faculties than throwing a ball to someone who is running at variable angles and distances from us. The only difference is the adjustment of timing that necessary to allow for modest speed of the ball compared with the high speed of the shot. Of course the hard part, in the early stages of learning to shoot, is *knowing* when the lead looks right to you. You can see this with the new shooter, who, as he becomes increasingly frustrated with a shooting *at* a 20 yard crossing shot, his coach tells him to "miss the next one three feet in front." and Bingo! The target breaks convincingly. Of course the new student is amazed and if he's a smart student, he remembers what he saw and learns to break the target again by applying the same bird/barrel relationship.

At the other end of the spectrum, watch a reasonably experienced guy, a good dove shot for example, shoot a 60 yard crosser on a sporting clay course. If that particular shot doesn't exist in his repertoire of sight pictures, he won't hit many, if *any* of them at first. Unless, of course, he has an experienced coach standing behind him telling him where he needs to shoot.

CHAPTER 4

"That Looks About Right to Me"

In the Scottish Highlands, the bleak and barren landscape is criss-crossed with ancient rock walls, called "drystane dykes" to stop the sheep and cattle from straying. These walls are constructed from locally available, irregular shaped rocks and each of these is placed in position without any cement or mortar. The wall is held together by a special, unique construction method and by its own weight. Each stone must be carefully selected by size and shape to ensure that it has a large contact area with its neighbor, so that over time, it does not slip. These walls date back centuries. They're not unique to Scotland and you can see other ancient walls, straddling hills and valleys across areas of Europe.

The guys that build these walls are superb craftsmen. An expert "drystane dyker" is a rare breed. After a long apprenticeship, they develop an "eye" for judging the shape and contour of a specific piece of rock so precisely, that when they pick one up, it fits perfectly into the gap in the wall. The amazing thing is, they become so good at doing this, they never pick a rock up then change their mind and lay it down again, to discard it for another one. Never. They simply eye the wall, eye the pile of rocks, identify a particular rock in the pile that looks about right and place it in its position on the wall. It's a bit like doing a complex, three dimensional jig-saw puzzle. I've watched these guys at work many times and it's skillful work, amazing to see. They just know that by visually measuring and judging the size of the rock, that particular piece will fit into that particular gap in the wall and it will be such a perfectly snug fit next to its neighbors that it looks almost as though it must have grown there! And that is *exactly* where the comparison with successful shotgunning comes in. When it comes to giving a specific target the correct amount of lead, the top guys know how big their piece of rock should be.

Every competitive shot-gunner, just like the guys building the wall, must be able to visually recognize a specific gap between the target and muzzles of his gun. It's called a target/barrel relationship or a bird /barrel relationship. Otherwise, as he triggers the shot, how would he know how far in front of the target his barrels were? This is a necessary requirement to allow for him to be able to successfully repeat the shot. But he must be able to do this without looking at the end of the gun. Some people mistake this for measuring. Well, I've got news for you. This *is* a game of measuring. Who says so? Well besides me, how about arguably one of the most successful coaches in the US at this time Dan Carlisle? Dan tells his students to "stretch it out to two inches, or three inches," whatever the case may be for the lead on the particular target. Isn't that a form of measuring? Of course but don't confuse this "seeing" the correct bird/barrel relationship with "checking" the correct bird/barrel relationship by glancing back at the bead or end of the gun. This is what true "measuring" is; and it's the kiss of death for successful shot gunning. Why? Because the human eyes don't work like that. The eyes can only focus on one thing at a time and if we attempt to focus on two things that are in the same "frame" but moving at different speeds (i.e. the moving end of the gun and a fast moving clay target) we will miss as we glance back at the end of the gun because the gun will stop as we do this. All the lead will then "evaporate" and a miss behind is the result.

Try this simple test. As you read this chapter, look at an object in the room, any object, door knob, light switch, it doesn't matter. Now quickly point your finger at it. The point is perfect every time isn't it? And you did it without looking at the end your finger didn't you? Now do the same again but this time, point an inch to the right, or an inch to the left, or three inches to the right or left, once again it doesn't matter. Decide how far you will point in front *before* you actually do it; in other words, say to yourself; "this time I will point two inches to the left, or right as the case may be." By pointing a pre-determined distance in front of the object, you are, in effect, *giving it some lead.* Usually, the first point is the correct one, we seldom need to "adjust" and reposition the finger do we? So why should pointing with a shotgun be any different? It isn't; *providing we first serve "an apprenticeship" to teach us exactly where we must point.* Once we can learn to do this, in other words, once we see the correct bird/barrel relationship, we must pull the trigger immediately. We should not "poke and hope" but also we should not "track" the target. We must shoot intuitively.

Many years ago in the UK I was coaching a lady on a skeet field. She just didn't get it and shot directly *at* the target every time. Of course, on the narrow angle shots, because of the width of the shot pattern, she did hit some of the targets…. but she missed more than she hit. When she then moved to the center stations i.e. the full crossers, she couldn't hit any of them. I needed something that she was familiar with, to use to demonstrate to her the amount of lead she needed to break the target. So, taking her gun and putting it in the gun rack, I asked her to show me how long she thought a loaf of bread was. The lady looked puzzled; (what exactly had this got to do with shot-gunning?) but then she indicated, by holding her hands apart, about 10-12 inches. This was many years ago in the UK you understand and at that time a standard white loaf was about 11 inches long.

"OK," I said, "Have you got a good imagination?"

The lady appeared to be slightly hesitant, wondering what was coming next but she nodded her head.

"This time, I don't want you to shoot *at* the target. I want you to shoot (we were standing on #1 and this was the low house target) the length of a loaf in front of it."

The lady looked perplexed but, with a shrug of her shoulders, removed her gun from the rack and loaded a shell in the lower chamber.

As she called for the target and started her move onto the line to intercept it, I was watching over her shoulder. This time, instead of shooting *at* the target, I could see that the gun was positioned a small amount in front of it as she pulled the trigger.

"Bang!" the first target broke convincingly and so did the next four. The lady was elated.

We moved to #2, wider angle and the range was slightly more. More lead was required and I said;

"Do the same here but now give this target two loaves"

The lady obliged and several more targets broke convincingly.

On #3, (which is a full crossing shot on a skeet field) I asked the lady to give the target a 4 loaf lead. At first she looked at me in disbelief and said;

"Four loaves? Surely not!"

"Trust me," I said "four loaves" and sure enough the target broke.

Now if we do the actual physics on the lead requirement from #3 on a skeet field, the lead we need is 3 feet 9 inches, or 45 inches. The lady had already told me that she thought a loaf was about 10 or 11 inches long. Four loaves was 44 inches, which was pretty close. So by giving this lady something that she was familiar with and then converting this into the leads on a skeet field that *I knew to be correct*, she was able to break the targets. In other words, I knew by experience where the lady's gun should be relative to the target and now, from my demonstration, so did she.

My experience with the lady on the skeet field many years ago started me thinking.

If the loaf of bread theory worked for her, would it work for other shooters? Sometimes it does. But as always, with shotgunning it's often a case of different strokes for different folks. Some shooters, especially in the early stage of learning to shoot, have difficulty "projecting" lead, out there at the target. This is because of the phenomenon of perspective. The word "perspective" means the effect of distance (range) by means of which the eye judges spatial relationships. Perspective, especially at extended range targets, plays a big part in the outcome of a successful shot.

So I would like to tell you another story. Some years later I was coaching another client, also on a skeet field. I tried the "give this target about one foot approach" on # 1 and it worked, probably because of the narrow angle of the target and the wide pattern. But on the middle stations, where he needed about four feet of lead, try as he might, he just couldn't connect. So we went back to the #1 low house target and I asked him to move his gun smoothly onto the line of the target and when he saw a small "gap" in front of the target, to trigger the shot.

"How much of a gap?" came the inevitable question.

"Oh not very much, about the width of my little finger" and having said that I held my finger next to the end of his muzzles, (of course, the gun was unloaded at this stage!) indicating where the target should be as he triggered the shot. Once again, this visual indication worked really well and the client started to break the targets. Then we went back to the full crosser on the center station and this time I held my hand up next to his barrels.

"This time," I said "give the target four fingers."

His eyebrows raised noticeably but he loaded the gun.

"Pull!" he called and I held my breath as he moved the smoothly gun to intercept the target My ploy worked and the target broke convincingly. So, what's the point of the two stories? Simply this. Some shooters see lead at the target, some see it at the muzzle. It doesn't matter, so long as he understands what he, as an individual, sees. And there's another interesting point worth mentioning here. The more accomplished the shooter is, the more he is likely to say he sees the lead out there in feet at the target. I have no scientific explanation for this

After this experience, I wrote a small instructional skeet book called "Skeet Shooting, a new perspective for the beginner." Over a period of several months, dozens of calculations and experiments involving pieces of string, bits of wood and countless shots on a skeet field, I came up with a formula. In the book, I described what I called a "unit" method for applying lead *in inches at the muzzle* to skeet targets. It works very well. *Skeet Shooting* is now out of print but the formula is in the skeet section of my book *Successful Shotgunning*.

So if we can see lead in terms of units at the barrel end on a skeet field, can we then take this a step further and use a similar method on a sporting clay course? Can we also make some sort of correlation as to what these units will correspond to in feet out there at the target and if we *can* do this, won't the process of applying lead be simplified? It seems to be; this method works well. It helps shooters to establish a repertoire of sight pictures and by doing this, they punch up in class very quickly.

But hold on a minute. Presuming we can learn how to do this, which shooting method should we use to apply it? Isn't *that* one of the secrets to becoming a good shot? Not really and let me explain why. It's a recognized fact that sustained or constant lead is the method used by more competition shooters than any other, with pull away coming in second. So why does George Digweed use a controlled swing through technique? He's a World Champion, doesn't this seem to suggest that a controlled swing through shooter will hit more targets if he uses a swing through technique? I doubt it. What about Dan Carlisle? He favors pull-away. Does he break more targets because of it? Probably not. Scott Robertson, Bobby Fowler and others swear by sustained or constant lead and they all hit more than their share of targets, so what's the deal? More importantly, which method is best? The answer is none of the above and all of the above, because believe it or not, all the top guys use the same shooting method.

The same method, I hear you say? How can that be if George favors swing-through, Dan likes pull-away and Bobby prefers sustained lead? Because we're talking about different methods of *gun movement* here, *not* visual lead. All these guys have developed, over a period of time, what I call muzzle and trigger "patience" and they pull the trigger at exactly the split second that the bird/barrel relationship light comes on for them regardless of the speed of their gun. I call it TLAR. The "that looks about right to me shooting method."

So I have a question for the experienced shots that are reading this book. How many times have you pulled the trigger on a particular target, or a dove that's skimming the across the top of a sunflower field and in the split second between the gun going off *but before the shot pattern reaches the target*, you just *know* that you will hit it? That's exactly the sort of thing that I'm talking about.

CHAPTER 5

The "Unit" lead system for sporting clays.

Picture the scene. A shooter runs the station and as he exits the safety cage, what's the question that his shooting buddies always ask? You've guessed it: - "How much lead did you see?" Since sportsmen used crude shotguns to intercept moving targets centuries ago, more has been written about one subject than any other: - forward allowance. For most of us, that illusive element "lead" is always the "frustration factor," isn't it? As far as I know, nobody has ever written a book that approaches the subject of applying a specific lead to a specific target, until now.

Lead is more difficult to evaluate than line, because it is determined by three factors: - angle, speed and distance. New shooters can easily become overwhelmed with all the variables they need to consider for successful interception of moving targets. With sporting clay targets, because of the diversity of the presentations, this is complicated; everybody struggles initially with first visually calculating and then mentally implementing the correct amount.

If it were easy to mathematically gauge the variables of angle, speed and distance that we need to intercept a moving target with a cloud of pellets, we would all shoot with unerring accuracy and there would be no need to write books of this sort. Sure, we all know that targets are moving and if we don't shot in front of them, we aren't going to hit many but the hard part is deciding *exactly how far* you need to point in front of the target, to score a hit. That's the difference between a good shot and a not-so-good shot isn't it? The top guys see "x" amount of lead and the target breaks. The inexperienced shooter sees "y" and it doesn't.

It's exactly the same with compound lead targets, a chondel, for example, that requires both horizontal and vertical lead. Your coach may tell you that the target, in a certain area, is dropping and you must shoot underneath it- but he doesn't tell you *how far* underneath it you must shoot, does he? Frustrating, isn't it? So, if I could show you a method, based on the laws of physics, the effects of perspective, trigonometry and ballistics, that we could use to apply a *simplified* visual indication (bird/barrel relationship) of precisely how much lead we need, would that sound like a good deal to you? In other words, a logical way to apply the correct amount of lead to each target, (that actually works!), without going through a head-scratching dilemma every time we see a different presentation? Sporting Clay shooters need specifics and that's why I developed this method. It works well; I have been perfecting it for several years now and teaching it to my students. Once mastered, it's the only method you will need to break every target on a sporting clay course.

For competitive shot gunning, as I said in the earlier chapter, we need to see lead either in inches at the muzzle or feet at the target, there is no other way. Then, if we are successful with this visual assessment and the target breaks, we also need to remember exactly what bird/barrel relationship we saw and take a "mental picture" so that we then have the ability to repeat the shot. So, which of these methods is quicker and easier to learn, lead in inches at the muzzle or feet out there at the target? In my experience, in the early stages of learning "what looks right," identifying a bird/barrel relationship at the muzzle end is much easier *for most of us*. Why? Because a miniscule amount of lead at the gun end, translates into several feet at the target end and by applying lead in this way, we don't need to consider the (sometimes confusing) phenomenon of perspective. The word "perspective" means the effect of distance (range) by means of which the eye is able to judge spatial relationships.

The effects of perspective present all sporting clay shooters a target evaluation dilemma at some stage, especially at extended ranges. We can see this clearly on a long fast crossing target thrown for a high tower. Because the target is silhouetted against the back-drop of the sky, with no familiar objects in the same "frame" to help with judging speed and distance, the target appears top be moving much slower than it actually is.

Our lead requirements on the infinite variety of targets we encounter on a sporting clay course may be anywhere from 0 feet of angular lead on the straight away targets, to over 15 feet or more on the long, 60 yard plus shots, with all the myriad of combinations in between. Think about long crossers, for example. It is difficult initially, for most of us the get a good "feel" of lead *in feet* out there at the target, especially on the long shots. Try telling a sporting clay shooter that on a 60 yard, 40 mph, 90 degree crossing target thrown from a high tower that he needs to apply 14 to 15 feet of lead out there at the target and he won't have the slightest idea what you are talking about. But if that same guy can establish, in his visual repertoire of sight pictures, what a "unit" of lead looks like at the end of his gun instead of how much lead he needs at the target end, it becomes easier.

As he practices applying different lead requirements on the easier shots, from experience, he learns that if he gives a 20 yard crossing shot about 4 units, (about 3 inches at the muzzle) the target will break. Now, it becomes very easy for him give this 60 yard target visually ½ as much again. If he now gives the 60 yard target 6 units, my guess is that there will be a very good chance that it also, will break. In other words all he needs to do is re-evaluate the additional range (to allow for the shot deceleration) and he now has a *logical* way to apply more lead, without guessing and missing with his first few shots. He doesn't have to be exact either, because on many shots, his pattern will compensate and save the day.

To better understand how this method works so successfully, let's do some calculations. The time of flight it takes of a 7 ½ shot size shell with an initial muzzle velocity of 1,200/1,250 feet per second to travel certain distances is as follows:

10 yards – 0.027 of a second
20 yards – 0.060 of a second
30 yards – 0.097 of a second
40 yards – 0.139 of a second
50 yards – 0.186 of a second
60 yards – 0.238 of a second.

Most targets fall some where between the speeds of 30 mph and 50 mph. and if we do the calculations on a standard target that is moving at *approximately* 30 mph the actual lead requirement that the laws that the laws of Physics dictate that is necessary to provide successful interception with a column of No. 7 ½ shot on a full crossing shot is: - 2.64 feet at 20 yards, 4.62 feet at 30 yards and 5.56 feet at 40 yards. The calculations on the 40 mph target would be 3.52 feet at 20 yards, 5.69 feet at 30 yards and 8.15 feet at 40 yards. The 50 mph target would need 4.39 feet at 20 yards, 7.11 feet at 30 yards and 10.192 at 40 yards.

In actual shooting situations in the field we can't be as specific as this and before all the mathematicians get their slide rules and calculators out and tell me that it is hopeless to try to calculate and then apply actual *accurate* linear measurements to leads on clay targets, I would agree completely. In fact recently, someone came up with a computer program that will accurately calculate the precise lead we need to see at various angles and distances using shells of various velocities. There is nothing new in this and occasionally these "foolproof methods" bubble to the surface. The problem is that they don't work because of the "human" element. The shooter still needs to evaluate range. He also needs to evaluate the angle. He also needs to evaluate the speed of the target. These things only come from experience out in the field. Also, the 20 yard shot is never going to be *exactly* 20 yards away. A 40 mph target is never going to be moving at *exactly* 40 mph. Although we may be attempting to shoot these targets with a sustained or constant lead method, gun speed also, will vary slightly. The speed of the shot and the speed of the targets are variables that we have very little control over control over but remember also that the shotgun is a forgiving weapon. We always have a small advantage with shot string on the close targets and a large advantage with width of the pattern.

For the purpose of simplification, if we take a target that is a full crossing shot (90 degrees to the shooter) *approximate* lead would be 3.5 feet at 20 yards, 5.5 feet at 30 yards and 8.5 feet at 40 yards. Practical application with research in the field has proved these lead requirements to be realistically accurate for our purposes. At 50 yards, the lead for a full crosser is 10 feet 9 inches and at 60 yards it is 14 feet 10 inches.

While we're on the subject of ballistics, a common myth that exists with sporting clay shooters is that they can give a target less perceived lead by using a faster shell. They can, marginally....but the trade-off is the felt recoil. With a 7 ½ shot size shell with a muzzle velocity of approximately 1,300 feet per second, the leading pellets in the shot column would reach the target with a remaining velocity of 680 feet per second. These pellets would take approximately 0.132 of a second to reach a 40 yard target. A slower shell, 1145 feet per second for example, would take 0.146 of a second to reach a 40 yard target. The difference in lead would be the amount that the target would travel in the difference between the two shot flight times i.e. 0.014 of a second. The actual difference in lead would be the amount of time it takes the target to travel in this time interval, which is only a few inches and this is only on a full crossing shot. Quartering or narrow angle targets would be a lot less.

The "exponential" effect

From the calculations above we can see that, because the shot charge is slowing down rapidly as the range increases, on a full crossing shot, the 40 yard target (at 40 mph) doesn't need twice the lead assumed for the 20 yard target but more than this. The 60 yard shot at 40 mph would need, not 10.5 feet (three times the lead assumed for the 20 yard shot) but approximately 14 feet 10 inches of lead, *over 4 times the lead that the 20 yard target needed.* This is because the shot charge, that starts off at approximately 1,200 ft/second, takes about 0.06 seconds to travel 20 yards; 0.097 of a second to travel 30 yards and 0.139 of a second to travel 40 yards and four times as long to get to the 60 yard target. In other words, the shot column simply takes longer to get there and the lead requirement doesn't increase with a liner relationship, it is *exponential.*

As range increases and the exponential effect comes into play, the familiar constant angle we can apply to many of the close shots is no longer adequate. This is why, *on the full crossing shots*, the ability to judge range is more important. So, if the effect of range slows the shot down considerably, this must mean that as the target gets further away from us, we must apply more and more lead to connect with it doesn't it? That's correct. However, for angle targets, other than full crossers, this does not mean (as most of us would suspect), that this will proportionally increase *visually* by very much at the gun end, so the effect of perspective is minimized. Today, on a testing sporting clay course, 60 yard targets and in some cases even longer shots that this, are by no means uncommon and this is where, for many of us, the application of lead becomes more complicated. But it doesn't need to be if you use this system.

If we do some more calculations, a narrow angle target, at approximately 15 degrees to our shooting position requires the following lead at the muzzle:

Distance to the target	Lead seen in inches at the muzzle.
20 yards	0.7
30 yards	0.8
40 yards	0.8
50 yards	0.9
60 yards	1.0

The actual lead we need for successful interception at the target end (not the perceived lead) may be anything from 3 ½ feet on the 20 yard target, to nearly 15 feet on the 60 yard shot. Because of the narrow angle, the perceived lead will be approximately 2 feet 6 inches on the 20 yard target to 3 feet 8 inches on the 60 yard shot. But the difference in the lead requirement *at the muzzle* between the 20 yard and the 60 yard target is only 3/10 ths of an inch. So does this mean that if we give *any* target that is either incoming or outgoing a bird/barrel relationship at the muzzle of somewhere between 0.7 of an inch to 1.0 inch that we should break the target? As amazing as this seems, that is correct. It also means that because of the beneficial effect of the width of our shot column, that we can apply a specific measurement at the muzzles that would work on *all* the narrow angle shots (either incoming or outgoing) and because of this, the process of applying lead would be simplified.

Ah ha! I can almost hear the mathematicians saying again. This is on the narrow angle shots. What about a wide angle shot at say, at approximately 45 degrees to the shooter? Once again, one bird/barrel relationship on this target would still work, *providing we make a good interpretation of the angle of the target relative to our shooting position*. If we do the calculations on this target, the lead seen at the muzzles would be:

Distance to the target	Lead seen in inches at the muzzle
20 yards	1.9 inches
30 yards	2.1 inches
40 yards	2.3 inches
50 yards	2.5 inches
60 yards	2.7 inches

As the angle increases so does the lead requirement and in order to successfully intercept this particular target, the perceived lead we would need would be from approximately 2 feet 4 inches on the 20 yard shot, to 10 feet 2 inches on the 60 yard shot, a difference of about 8 feet. But the difference *at the muzzle* would only be 0.8 inches between the 20 yard and 60 yard shots. Why? Because the lead at the muzzle would be approximately 1.9 inches for the 20 yard shot, to 2.7 inches for the 60 yard shot. Once again, due to the width of our pattern, (and this would still be approximately 30 inches wide at 60 yards with an improved modified choke) this means that we can apply a specific amount of lead at the muzzle (in this case 3 units) that would allow us to break any target at an approximate 45 degree angle to our shooting position *at any range*.

The "unit" system

So what exactly is a "unit" of lead and exactly how did I arrive at this illusive measurement? Over a long period, I did many calculations and experiments, both on a skeet field and sporting clay course. I needed to come up with a visual "common denominator," something that my students could apply to each target at variable angles and ranges, which would then correlate into feet at the target, without this being too complicated. Without going into a boring and lengthy explanation, what I found was this. For the purpose of simplification, let's assume that we use a standard shell of approximately 1,200 to 1,250 feet per second. Let's say we have a 30 yard, full crossing target that comes off the throwing plate of an automatic target launcher at 40 mph. 40 mph is 58.66 feet per second. The shot column will take (7 ½ shot) 0.06 seconds to get to the target which means that the lead required will be *approximately* 5 feet 8 inches. At the muzzles, this looks like *approximately* 3 inches. If we divide this by 4 we get 0.75 of an inch.

Based on my experiences with the shooters in the earlier chapter I realized that the visual indication, (the bird/barrel relationship "common denominator" if you like) that we are looking for is *approximately* ¾ of an inch; roughly the width of a one cent piece, something that we are all familiar with. This measurement at the gun end doesn't need to be exact; it's just a brief, visual indication as we make our move to intercept the target, between the side of the muzzle and the target as we trigger the shot. Once you get used to applying it, it becomes remarkably easy, especially as we use it to correlate the leads on the longer shots.

Now the next part will surprise many of you. By using this unit system of visualizing lead at the muzzles, (providing we make a reasonably good interpretation of the approximate angle and decide what category the target falls into *before* we shoot it) there are only 6 bird/barrel relationship lead pictures that we need to apply *to every target presentation we find on a sporting clay course with* a standard lead requirement out to ranges of about 50/60 yards. How can that be? Because this is the best part; this is where, when using this method on all the angular targets, the phenomenon of perspective and the need to interpret range is inconsequential.

Let's say we have a target that is quartering away from us. The machine is to our left and the target is a 7 o'clock to 12 o'clock, or a **narrow angle** target at about 15 degrees to our shooting position. The area we intend to break this target is about 20 yards away. At 20 yards the calculations show that this target will need a visual lead of approximately 0.7 inches at the barrel. One "unit" is about 0.75. By using a sustained lead method, if we give this target **1 unit** of lead, the target will break. If we then back up ten yards and now shoot this same target *at the same angle* at 30 yards we will still break it with a 1 unit lead (the calculations show that this target will need 0.8 inches of lead) and the same one unit out to 40 yards and further.

Now what about a narrow angle incoming shot? If the target, *in the area we intend to shoot it*, is quartering in at an approximate angle of 15 degrees to our shooting position the lead will still be one unit. And the other amazing thing is, on these incoming or outgoing angled shots, making a conscious evaluation of range isn't necessary. So, am I saying that on an incoming target that is coming towards us at a narrow angle (like, for example a low #1 on a skeet field) and we give it a one unit lead at the muzzle, the target will break? That's correct. Am I also saying that if we then have another target at the *same angle* to our shooting position, coming from a high tower that is 60 yards away and again we give this target a one unit lead *at the muzzle* this target will also break? As amazing as it may seem, that is correct.

Think of the spokes of a bicycle wheel for a moment. If we are standing in the center of the wheel and we draw two imaginary lines, one from the pupil of our master eye (or the eye above the rib) and the other along the rib of the gun out to the target, the amount of lead increases proportionally at the target end as the range increases. This means, in effect, that if we give a narrow angle target a small amount of lead at the muzzles, the lead at the target will increase more substantially as a result. You can see from diagram 4 (page 28) that there is no necessity to substantially increase the visual lead at the gun end on these angle shots.

"Ah hah!" I can hear the mathematicians say. "That's incorrect. If the target is further away, then we *must* need more lead to intercept it." I agree; *mathematically* they would be correct but *visually*, in other words the amount of the "gap" they need to see at the muzzles of the gun, one unit would still work on these narrow angle targets. Of course, as the target gets further away we may now need to shoot slightly underneath it, (more about this later) but the *angular* lead will visually remain more or less the same. Now let's do the calculations on the lead we need on an **intermediate** angle that is going out at approximately 8 o'clock to 12 o'clock, in other words, at approximately 30 degrees to our shooting position. The calculations show that we would need approximately 1 foot 9 inches feet of lead, if we shot this target with a shell with a velocity of 1,200 ft/second. The lead seen in inches at the muzzle would be about 1.4 inches. If we apply the unit method to this target we would need 2 units or approximately 1.5 inches. Don't forget that on this target our shot pattern would be about 24 to 30 inches so if we shot the target with 2 units of lead at the muzzle, it should break. Once again, if this same target is shot *at the same angle* but now at 30 yards, the calculations would reveal that we would need 2 feet 10 inches but at the muzzle we would see 1.5 inches, exactly 2 units. At 40 yards the calculations would be 4 feet 2 inches at the target but about 1.7 inches at the gun. Once again the two unit lead would work. Now look at the same target at 60 yards. The figures on this show that we would need 7 feet 5 inches of lead *out there at the target* but at the muzzle end of the gun we would only need 2.0 inches, in other words a very modest increase if ½ an inch. But at the gun end and due to the combination of the "bike wheel" effect and pattern *the two unit lead would still work for us on this target.*

So, what about the wide angle shots? This target is going out at somewhere between 9 o'clock and 10 o'clock to 12 o'clock, or approximately 45 to 60 degrees to our position. If we shoot this target the lead we need to see at the muzzles would be about 1.9 inches of lead. For the same target at 60 degrees we would need about 2.3 inches of lead. The average between the two is 2.1 inches at the muzzle. If we use the unit system we would need to give this target about 3 units. If we first shoot this target at 20 yards, the calculations show that the lead we need at the target end is about

2 feet 6 inches. At the muzzle it would be approximately 2 inches. A 3 unit lead is about 2.25 inches (0.75 x 3) so we should break the target with a three unit lead. Once again, if this same target is shot at 30, 40 50 and further, the 3 units would still work. How can that be? Because as the target gets further away the calculations at 60 yards show lead at the target would be approximately 10 feet 6 inches at the same angle so our 3 unit lead would still work. This sounds almost too good to be true doesn't it? I agree; but I can assure you that this method does work. So if we can apply both one and two unit and three unit leads to the angles, what about the full crossing shots? What units do we apply to these? This is what works. Any target that is at an angle of approximately *more* than about 60 degrees to your shooting position *in the area you intend to shoot it* would be classified as a full crossing shot. On full crossers, we need to consider the exponential effect. This is what works on these shots:

15 to 20 yard crossing shot	4 units
20 to 30 yard crossing shot	4 units
30 to 40 yard crossing shot	5 units
40 to 50 yard crossing shot	5 units
50 to 60 yard crossing shot	6 units

As I have already said, range and angle are the variables that have the biggest impact on the outcome of the shot (especially on the full crossing shots) and because of this, a reasonably accurate assessment must be made *before we take the shot.* Range is difficult for most of us to judge at first, but on these full crossing shots, when in doubt it is best to err on the forward side. If we are too far in front we may still break the target with the tail end of our shot column. If we are a millionth of an inch behind the target we will miss.

So why do I suggest using a 4 unit lead on both the 15 to 20 yard crossing shot and the 20 to 30 yard crossing shot? Because we have two variables to consider as we trigger the shot. These are the slight differences in gun speeds and shooter reaction time. But the "margin of error" with these two variables should be compensated for by the width of the pattern. Using a skeet choke, the pattern width at 15 yards would be about 20 inches but almost twice this (38 inches) at 30 yards. By the same rule the pattern from an improved modified choke at 20 yards (approx.18 inches) would be more than twice this (42 inches) at 40 yards. The more experienced shots become so precise when they shoot that they have the ability to "tailor" a target. What this actually means is that, by using a sustained lead method, their gun speed is synchronized exactly with the speed of the target. If they take the front edge or back edge off the target, they can then adjust their sight picture so that, with the next shot, they center it.

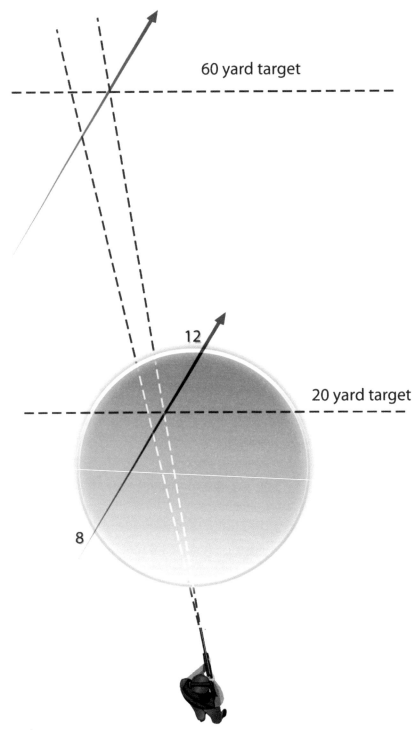

60 yard target

20 yard target

12

8

Diagram 4

In this example, the target is an intermediate angle requiring two units. If the bird/barrel relationship *at the muzzle* is projected out to the target at extended range, this two unit lead would still work, due to the "bike wheel" effect.

Now before all the mathematicians out there get their slide rules out again and tell me this is incorrect, don't forget that these figures are approximations. But if we do decide to calculate the leads seen at the muzzles on these targets, we would find that this "unit" system of applying leads would come remarkably close to the actual measurements that Physics dictates we would need in feet at the target or inches at the muzzle. For a 40 mph crossing shot using a 1,200 ft/sec shell, this is what we get:

15 to 20 yard target   2.73 inches at the muzzle (so 4 units or 3 inches would work)

20 to 30 yard target   3.02 inches at the muzzle (so 4 units or 3 inches is exactly right)

30 to 40 yard target   3.31 inches at the muzzle (so 5 units or 3.75 inches would work)

40 to 50 yard target   3.62 inches at the muzzle (so 5 units or 3.75 inches would work)

50 to 60 yard target   3.95 inches at the muzzle (so 6 units or 4.50 inches would work)

Practical applications, using a constant or sustained lead technique have proved that the application of these units at these range of targets are realistically accurate and very successful. Shooters who use these bird/barrel relationships punch up in class very quickly. Don't forget that we have the small advantage of shot string (especially on the closer targets) and the advantage (on all of them) of a shotgun's wide pattern. All these targets must be shot in the initial stages of learning the method, *by using a sustained lead method only*. The beauty of sustained lead shot is that, *at the moment the shot is triggered*, the gun and target is synchronized. There is no residual gun movement like there would be with either a pull-away or swing through method. Lead changes by using a different shooting method would be too complicated to explain but eventually, you will develop the muzzle and trigger "patience" and regardless of the chosen shooting method, you will select the correct sight picture as you trigger the shot.

CHAPTER 6

The Clock Face

Perceived and actual lead

Of the three things (angle, speed and range) that we need to consider with identifying the correct forward allowance on a target, the angle has the biggest impact on the outcome of a successful shot. So first of all, let me explain the difference between *actual* lead and *perceived* lead. Actual lead is the amount of forward allowance that the laws of physics dictate that we need, to ensure that the target and shot column will intersect successfully. Perceived lead is the amount of lead the shooters *thinks he needs to see at the muzzle* as he makes a shot. The angle that the target travels along, relative to our shooting position, determines the perceived lead that we need to apply on that particular target. Perceived lead is only the same as required forward allowance on the 90 degree crossing shots. A clay target, traveling at *approximately* 40 mph at an *approximate* range of 20 yards and at an *approximate* angle of 90 degrees relative to our shooting position will need *approximately* 3 ½ to 4 feet of forward allowance. But the perceived lead, as this angle changes, is less. For example, this same target, seen at an angle of about 15 degrees or so will still need about 3 ½ to 4 feet to intercept it but the perceived lead would be about 1 foot at the target or about ¾ of an inch at the muzzle.

The Clock Face

Years ago, Andy McCloud, one of the guys that taught me to shoot told me with a grin that "You can't tell the time properly, lad!" He then went on to explain how mentally visualizing the face of a clock, (something we are all familiar with since a very early age), can help many of us to very quickly learn perceived lead requirements when we shoot birds in the field. Andy went on to explain to me that if we try to imagine a clock face, laid out flat on the ground in front of us and we are standing at 6 o'clock, the seven o'clock to 1 o'clock bird, (either incoming or outgoing) was a "pigeon's wing" lead, the 8 o'clock to 2 o'clock shot was a "duck wing" lead and the 9 o'clock to 3 o'clock shot was a "goose wing" lead. Of course, all Andy was saying, in simplistic terms, was that as the angle increases, so does the perceived lead. The comparison worked; in a hunting situation, it was easy for me to apply this simple (but effective) strategy to birds in the field and hit more of them. Many coaches in the UK use this simple "clock face" as a visual aid for demonstrating target angles to their students and there are three ways that this "clock face" application can be useful to us when we shoot.

As we have already discussed, learning to read target angles is easiest on a skeet field and there is absolutely no doubt in my mind that this is the best way for the new shooter. The first skeet field was circular; in fact the game of skeet was originally called "round the clock". On a sporting clay course however, because of the variations in the topography and the trees, bushes etc, sometimes evaluating the angles may not seem quite as easy. But with practice, it becomes easier. We can use three basic angles on the skeet field for our lead requirements. For sporting clays, because of the diversity of presentations and greater ranges involved compared to a skeet field, I like to take this a step further, be more precise and use four angles. These are: - **narrow angle, intermediate**, **wide angle** and **full crossing shots.** A straight incomer and outgoing target would obviously require zero angular lead.

First we need to categorize each target in the area where we intend to shoot it. Imagine the clock face, not in its normal vertical position but lying flat on the ground in front of you. In every case, imagine you are standing at six o'clock and straight in front is 12 o'clock. The position of the machine is often a good indication of the degree of angle of the target relative to your shooting position, in other words, (if the machine is on your left), the target enters the clock face at 7 o'clock (or at 5 o'clock if the machine is on your right) and then exits the clock face at approximately 12 o'clock then it would be a **narrow angle shot**, (Page 41, fig1) somewhere between 0 and 15 degrees to our shooting position. If it enters at 8 o'clock or (4 o'clock) and leaves at 12 o'clock it is now what I call an **intermediate angle shot**, (Page 41, fig 2) at about 30 degrees to our shooting position. If the target enters at 9 o'clock (or 3 o'clock) and leaves at 12 o'clock it falls into the category of a **wide angle shot**, (Page 41, fig 3) somewhere at approximately between 45/60degrees to our shooting position. Anything that is greater than 45/60 degrees up to a maximum of 90 degrees would be classified as a **full crossing shot** (Page 41, fig 4) Because the perception of lead varies as the angle varies, in a competitive environment, *it is worth taking the time to evaluate the angle as accurately as possible.*

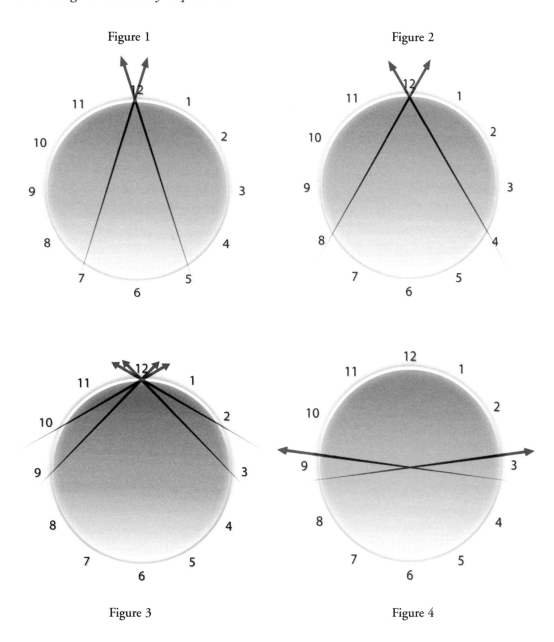

Figure 1

Figure 2

Figure 3

Figure 4

All these angle shots will be either opening angles or closing angles. What's the difference between the two? Let's look at the outgoing or closing angle targets first. Any target that is *outgoing* from your shooting position would be classified as a closing angle shot, in other words the angle relative to your position is *decreasing* as the target gets further away. This is where many shooters make a mistake.

"Ah ah!" they think. "The target is getting further away. Give it more lead." But they would be wrong with their assumption of this on the closing angle shots. Diagrams 5 and 6 illustrate this.

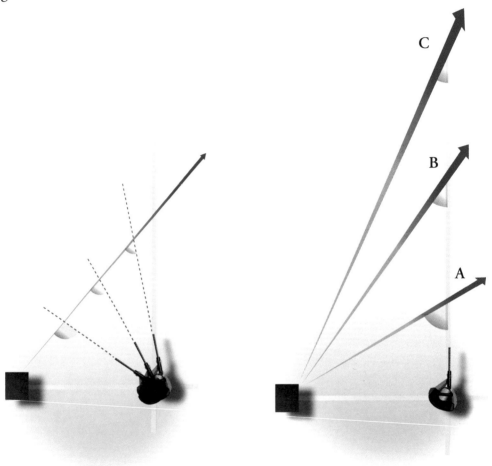

Diagram 5   Diagram 6

The angle of the target relative to our position dictates the lead requirement. In diagram 5, the place on the trajectory where we intend to take the target must be decided before we shoot. With diagram 6, target A requires *more* perceived lead than target C, even though target C is further away.

The opposite is true with the opening angles. Any target that is *incoming* would fall into the category of an opening angle shot, in other words the perceived lead will increase as the target gets nearer. When using the unit system of applying lead, you must identify *the area where you intend to shoot the target relative to your shooting position.* Of course, in a competitive environment, we should be doing this anyway. The unit lead requirements on the closing angles will change as the target gets further away. For example, in diagram 6 target A at about 20 yards away (at approximately 60 degrees to our shooting positon) may be a wide angle, target B at 30 yards (approximately 30 degrees) may be a intermediate and target C at 40 yards (at approximately 15 degrees) may be a narrow angle. By the same rule, if the target is an opening angle as it gets nearer to your shooting position, it may fall into the category of a full crossing shot and the units we need to connect with it will also increase. Diagram 7 illustrates this.

Diagram 7
Target A requires more perceived lead than target B

The second way this "clock face" visualization can also help us, is to more accurately define the line of a target and make sure that our gun is traveling accurately along this line. This time we must imagine the clock face in its (normal) vertical position. To illustrate this, let's say we have an edge on teal that is climbing steeply as it leaves the trap. If the machine is in the center of the clock face (or if the place where the target first appears) is in the center of the clock face, the target line is now easy to identify. Many shooters, when faced with an unusual angle, drop a shoulder and pull the gun off-line. Visualizing the clock face can often prevent this. Diagram 8 shows this. Also, any "driven" target can be approached in the same way. By "driven" I mean any target that is coming from in front of your shooting position and traveling over your head. The center station, #8 on a skeet field is one example of this and most skeet shooters miss these targets over the top. From the center station the high house bird will be moving along a 2 o'clock line relative to your position. The low house target will be a 10 o'clock line. I exactly the same way, the clock face is also useful with the targets from a high tower. By imagining that your shooting position is always at six o'clock, a really high target will come over at 11 o'clock or 1 o'clock. Lower birds will be on a 10 o'clock and 2 o'clock line respectively.

1 o'clock

Diagram 8

Line is more important than lead. By visualizing a clock face in its more usual, vertical position (ie. flat on a wall), this steeply climbing teal target prescribes an 1 o'clock line. Failure to accurately move the gun along this line will result in a miss.

Target speeds and transitions

The clock face can also be used to identify compound lead requirements and also target speeds. If a target enters the clock face at three o'clock and leaves at 9 'o clock, it would be categorized as a single plane target requiring lead in one direction only. This line would also indicate that the target is still under full power. If the target then enters at 3 o'clock and leaves at 8 o'clock, now it would require lead in two directions, both horizontally and vertically. But this transitional phase also indicates that there is a reduction in speed and we must reduce our lead accordingly, perhaps by a third of our initial lead requirement that would apply if this target were a full crosser under maximum power. This target would fall into the category of what I call a "rectangle" shot. If the target now enters at three and leaves at 7 o'clock, by the same rule now we would need even less horizontal forward allowance (perhaps only ½ of our original lead) and even more vertical lead. This type of transitional target is a good candidate for a "box" shot.

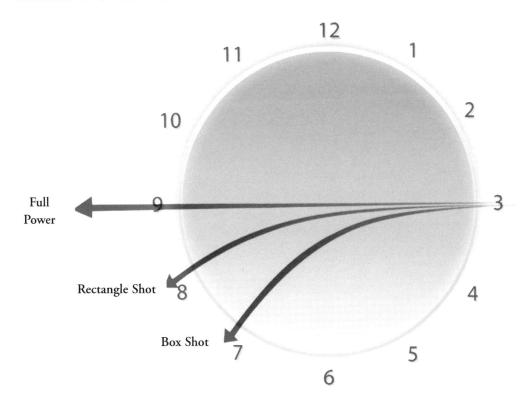

Diagram 9

CHAPTER 7

_____

Target Types

All airborne targets, due to the downward gravitational pull, prescribe a parabolic trajectory. The target rises, there is a period of transition and then it begins to fall. As soon as the target reaches the highest point of this parabolic curve, in other words, the transitional segment of its flight path, energy is bleeding off and the target is slowing down as a result. Without getting too much into the laws of Kinetic energy and aerodynamics, the distance the target travels and also the way in which it behaves as it prescribes this trajectory is proportional to its weight and its aerodynamic qualities. Simple. We all knew that didn't we? But hold on a minute.

Because we see more of them, our onboard computer registers that for the most of us the flight path of a standard target is the one that we are familiar with. When it is thrown from a machine in level flight, the standard target defines a reasonably predictable line. When we consider the specialty targets, reading the line on these may not be as straightforward as many of us think. Because of the diversity of target presentations that we encounter on a sporting clays course, this bleed off of energy may occur quicker in some targets and slower in others and as the weight of the target and aerodynamic qualities vary, so do the trajectories. Simply put, with specialty targets, different kinds have different lines.

Unlike Skeet and Trap and to make the game of sporting clays more interesting, there are a variety of targets on a sporting clay course. This in turn determines the choke and load selection we need to break them.

1. The standard target is 4 ½ inches in diameter, dome shaped and approximately 1 1/8 inches thick.
2. The midi is 3 ½ inches in diameter, 7/8 th inches thick also dome shaped. Visually, this target is the same shape as the standard but because the ratio of weight/ air cushion supporting the target is better than the standard the aerodynamic qualities of the midi are superior. Simply put, midis maintain their velocity and flight path better than standards.
3. The mini is 2 3/8 of an inch and for its size, has the biggest air cushion. Because of the lack of weight, however, it slows down quickly.

Target "vulnerability"

Clay targets that are designed for use as airborne targets are always dome shaped to give them lift as they fly through the air. This "domed" shape has three distinct areas of vulnerability that can (depending on the presentation) influence chokes and load combination.

1. The "shoulder" of the target is made stronger because this is the part of the target that comes in contact with the rubber on the arm of the clay target launcher. As the target accelerates from rest to somewhere over 50 mph the force exerted on this area is considerable. As the target rolls up the rubber strip of the trap arm during launching, approximately 12 inches or so of the shoulder comes into contact with this rubber strip and as it does so, the target spins as it leaves the throwing plate of the machine. This spin of the target in the early stage of its flight will also have the effect of deflecting shot from the shoulder area. To reduce breakage, the targets have been designed to compensate for this by building the shoulder thickness up. International trap targets, used in bunker trap machines (where target speeds are considerably faster than Skeet and Sporting Clays), are made slightly smaller and with an even thicker shoulder to compensate for this rapid acceleration from rest.

2. The convex "dome" of the target, when presented full-face to the shooter (as in a springing teal type presentation) is easier to break than the full shoulder presentation.

3. The concave underside if the target is the easiest of all to break.

Why is all this important? Because, in a competitive environment, we must consider the effects of synergism on some target presentations. A rough translation of synergy means the combination of two forces that produce a greater effect. In shotgunning terms this means that, if we take a trap-type shot (where the target is traveling directly away from us as an example), because the target and the shot column are both traveling in the same direction, the target will be harder to break. This is exactly the reason why trap shooters use tight chokes and 7 ½'s. If the target were coming towards us, the combination of the two forces would provide a "synergistic boost" and the target would be much easier to break. A more open choke and smaller shot size would break the same target at the same distance.

The battue t............................ profile, is the fastest target. Although the battue ...., compared to the standard, midi and mini, this .... the same "lift" as these targets and this makes the battu..................... Edge on to the shooters position and they are difficult to .... ow this next suggestion will surprise many of you. The easiest place to take a battue target is just as it starts to turn and present its full face, NOT after it has already turned and started to drop as most instructors will tell you. (**see figure 1**). Why? Because in this area we can still apply a "standard" lead and we only need to shoot in front of it. But you must have a "game plan" so that you know *exactly* where on the trajectory this transition is and exactly what lead you must apply as the target turns. A moment's hesitation with triggering the shot will allow the target to curl over and then we must apply a compound lead.

Battues are usually thrown at a fairly steep angle to the horizontal so that they "develop" correctly and roll over to present their full face. This is where they are easiest to see and this is why most people decide to take them as they do this. Watch a battue in flight and you will notice that as it does this, it starts its descent at approximately 45 degrees to the horizontal (**see figure 2**). Now the target needs both horizontal and vertical lead and many years ago I devised a simple method for breaking battues that works very well. I called it the "box shot". This is what works on the battue with a "standard" flight pattern. Let's say we have a battue that is coming from our right to our left. Look at the area where the battue "peaks" and begins to "roll" to

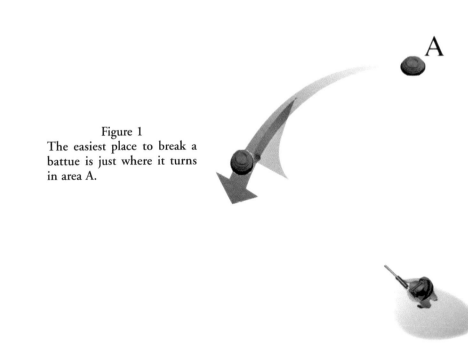

Figure 1
The easiest place to break a
battue is just where it turns
in area A.

45 degrees to
the horizontal

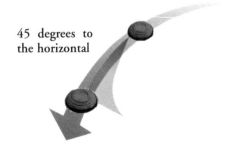

Figure 2
As the target begins to lose power,
it will drop at approximately 45
degrees to the horizontal.

start its descent. Your gun hold position should be just underneath the area where the target peaks and slightly to the right. The gun hold position is critical on this target, if you want to be consistent. A gun hold that is too far to the right will result in too much gun movement and the gun may stray outside the parabolic arc (**see figure A**). A gun hold that is too far to the left will mean you will attempt a "spot shot" at the target (**see figure B**) and although you may be successful with a close target because your wide pattern may "save the bacon," at extended range this is unadvisable.

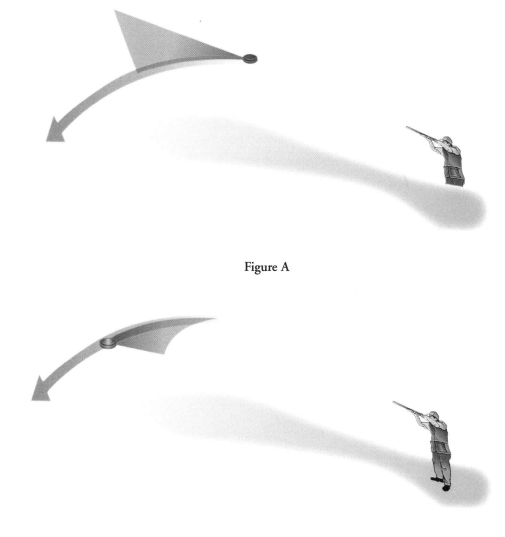

Figure A

Figure B

If this specific area is approximately 20 yards from your shooting position, try to imagine a 1 foot square box, out there at the target. When the target is in the top left hand corner of this box, shoot at the bottom right corner. At 30 yards, increase the size of the box to 2 feet. At 40 yards the box size should be approximately 3 feet. At the muzzle, for most shooters at 40 yards, this will translate into a 1 inch "box." Once again, the same exponential ballistic principles of the shot slowing down at extended range are what influence the box size and once learned, the "box shot" works very well and is very consistent. At extended range, as the shot takes longer to get to the target the only adjustment we make to the shot is to visually make the box bigger and we should score a hit. When using this method, it is essential to shoot each target on the same point on its trajectory and the only adjustment that should be made at extended range is that the box size must be increased. A battue at 50-60 yards, due to the exponential effect of the shot column slowing down, may need a visual indication of a 5 or 6 foot box or more.

In all cases (with a "looping" trajectory), the gun should move in empathy with the target, in other words the gun should be prescribing a "mirror image" of the parabolic curve of the battue. The gun must not be allowed to stray outside this parabolic arc. The muzzles must NOT be allowed to push outside the arc of the battues trajectory with a level swing (usually the result of an incorrect gun hold position and too much gun speed). An errant move with the muzzles outside the parabolic arc that the battue prescribes will mean it is now impossible to bring the muzzles back on line. This "box" method, although it works well with battues, is not restricted to them and can also be used in many situations with standard and midi targets. Any target that has an area on its trajectory where it is at approximately 45 degrees to the horizontal plane can be broken in the same way, providing we make an accurate calculation of the range involved. Many quartering-in targets, (thrown from a distant machine perhaps 80 yards away for example) will have a place on their trajectory where they visually fall at 45 degrees. At this point, they will break if the box method is used.

Best method

Sustained lead is the most consistent. Swing through and pull will work but if either of these methods is attempted, because of the curving flight line of the battue there is the possibility that the muzzles will stray outside this parabolic arc. The target will be missed outside the line.

Wind effect

Beware! The low weight of the battue at 76 grams combined with the absence of the deep concave profile makes the battue the most aerodynamically unstable of all the targets and wind interference can affect it more than we think. With a battue target coming from right to left and a sudden gust of wind from the same direction, the target may refuse to develop at all and never present its full face. With a gust from the opposite direction, it will climb steeply and then develop in a completely different place on its trajectory, catching the unprepared shooter off guard as it does this.

Chokes and loads

Battues are thin and at close range, up to 30 yards, open chokes and 8's will work well. Further than this 7 ½'s and light mod will still break them convincingly out to 50 yards or more.

CHAPTER 9

Chondels

The chondel target gives many shooters problems because the line is so deceptive, in fact I have many students that will book an hour or so, dedicating all the time to this type of presentation at various ranges and angles. Ten years ago, it was rare to see a chondel on a sporting clay course. The word "chondel" describes a specific aerobatics term. It relates to a maneuver where an aircraft executes a steep, climbing turn both to gain altitude and change direction simultaneously. In the sport of stunt flying, judges give points on a pilots ability to do this. With a perfectly executed chondel the pilot attempts to make a 180-degree directional turn, rapidly gaining altitude as he does this, eventually leveling out to end up flying in the opposite direction.

Of course we can't replicate this flight-path as accurately with a simple clay pigeon but the target that emulates the subtle curve of the chondel trajectory better than any other is the standard target, thrown at a steep angle from a canted machine. Machine manufactures have all been quick off the mark to develop and incorporate this modification in their machines to simulate and present this confusing target line. Most of them are now producing an in-built tilting mechanism in their machines to allow the course designer to do this better. In response to the call for more and more testing targets, we now have specialist machines that can throw not only the standard 108 mm target as a chondel in all its guises but also the heavier rabbit target from the same machine.

With any target presentation, the muzzles of the gun must move in empathy with the target to ensure successful interception. If either a true chondel or a looping rabbit are taken under power before the transitional part of the trajectory, the muzzle movement required to do this is easier, because it always easier to control the gun as we lift it than when we lower it. In other words, our mechanics will be better and more precise with the lifting motion. If a cunning course designer gives the shooter no alternative but to shoot the target after it transitions, he may have a problem with his muzzle management. If the muzzles of the gun are allowed to stray outside the parabolic curve of the trajectory (just as with the battue), even for an instant, a miss off-line may be the result.

The combination of this difficult gun movement, plus a target miss read usually spells disaster and a miss is certain. Chondels can be either be presented with either with the steeper "looping" trajectory (**see figure A**) or the flatter trajectory (**see figure B**). Because the target is presenting its "full face" there is an optical illusion; the target always appears nearer than it actually is. Because range is deceptive, line also can be a problem (the exponential effect) and many shooters miss behind and over the top. The "flat" trajectory chondel needs a lot of lead; especially if the heavier rabbit target thrown as a chondel, because there is no obvious "bleed off" of energy. A crossing rabbit chondel at 40-50 yards, for example, needs a full dose of a 5 to 6 unit lead to connect with it.

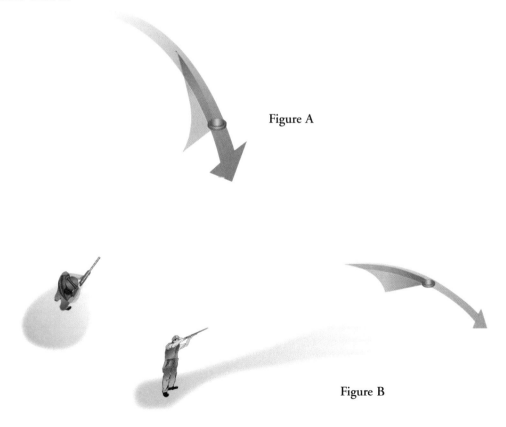

Figure A

Figure B

The "rectangle" lead works well with these flat trajectory chondels, either just before they peak or just as they level out and start to fall. The "box" lead method works well on the steeper, looping chondel either just before or just after it peaks.

Best method

Sustained lead is the best method to use here but there must be a "game plan" as to exactly where on the trajectory the intended break point is. A moments hesitation with triggering the shot may mean a hurried chase after the target and the gun may stray off the true target line. I have heard of a different technique that can be applied to a chondel where the gun is accelerated along a horizontal line relative to the target but (although some shooters use this method with some success) I don't recommend this method for consistency. Why? Because it contradicts one of the basic principles of successful shotgunning; the gun must move on the same line as the target.

Wind effect

Any target that is thrown with this looping trajectory is categorized as a chondel and this can mean a standard target, midi target or rabbit target. Each of them, because of the difference in weight and aerodynamic characteristics, can behave differently. Years ago, rabbit targets thrown on edge were called chondels by many people, but others (especially in the UK) called them "loopers." In effect, that's exactly what they are and with the heavy, rabbit target, deviation from the vertical line that they are thrown on, is influenced only slightly by wind interference for two reasons.

If we look at the physical characteristics of the rabbit target, first of all they are heavy which gives them more airborne stability. The auto rabbit target was designed to roll along the ground at high speed and also resist fragmenting by hitting small stones, bit of debris that it encounters as it does this. Although visually the same size as a standard target at 110 mm, it is thinner at 16mm but a lot heavier at 120 grams. Secondly they are and more robust to reduce breakage and (more or less) flat, without the convex or concave surface of the standard target.

The weight of the target influences the rate at which this slow down occurs and because of this, the parabolic curve of the standard target that is thrown as a chondel, will be completely different to the trajectory of the rabbit target in a similar presentation. The target with the most mass will respond less to this gravitational pull and the parabolic curve will be flatter for longer with the rabbit than the standard target. Also, because of the aerodynamic difference between the rabbit and standard, side wind will influence the line of the standard target far more than the rabbit target. Depending on from which side this wind interference occurs, a sudden puff of wind hitting either the convex or concave side of the target can dramatically influence the line and even more dramatically influence the range and as a result, the outcome of the shot. Ignore these subtle differences at your peril!

Chokes and loads

With full-face standard and midis improved cylinder and 8's work well out to 25-30 yards. Rabbits thrown as chondels need 7 ½'s at the same range. At ranges further than this and when standards and midis are thrown as angling away narrow angles, its best to tighten up a notch, modified and improved modified work well with 7 ½ shells.

CHAPTER 10

Taming the Teal

Springing what?" retorted the client, as I mashed the button and presented him with a testy pair of teal for his first time on a sporting clay course. "I ain't never seen any teal do that before!". That experience with teal targets was many years ago and of course that particular client's comments weren't unusual. Sporting clay targets are supposed to be representative of actual game bird shooting situations in the field but as the game of sporting clays gains popularity; in an effort to continually whet the insatiable appetites of the shooters; target presentations have become increasingly more complex. The evolution of the modern springing teal target is no exception and although wild teal do lift vertically for a second or two as they become airborne, this is greatly exaggerated with the simulated clay target version.

It's rare to find a pair of "predictable" teal targets because of the diversity of the presentation. If the targets are launched from a manual machine at a distance, the first will be rising and the second will often be falling in the place you intend to shoot it. We know that with any target, it is essential to get a good read and in this respect the teal can be tricky, especially the line. This is seldom exactly vertical and even is it is in the early stages of the trajectory, a teal target which is dropping, no longer has the stability of the spin as it comes off the throwing plate of the machine. This makes it much more susceptible to wind interference which will push the target off line quicker than almost any other target.

As I described in the section on reading the targets a narrow angle shot requires less lead, full crossing shot at 90 degrees more lead, but how do we know which category the teal target fits into? From automatic machines, teal targets can be launched at a variety of angles, from a fairly flat angle of 40 to 50 degrees, to some which are launched almost at 90 degrees, or as near to vertical as makes no difference. Course designers still drop these widely varying targets into the category of a springing teal, even though the flatter trajectory teal resembles a trap type-target. A clue is the amount of face or rim you can see on the targets. What do I mean by this? Just as perceived lead changes on a crossing target, the same is true of the teal. The flatter the profile or in other words, the more of the rim that is edge on to the shooter, the less lead the target requires, becoming in effect a trap type target. Diagram 11 explains this. Target A requires less perceived lead than target B.

The required sight picture as you trigger the shot on a teal target is almost the same as the driven shot off a high tower. The difference is that the teal rises almost vertically in front of you, instead of the target coming towards you and passing overhead, as it does with a driven target. The visual imagery is however, very similar, and this is what I tell my students. There are two methods we can use to shoot the teal, either swing through from behind, firing as the target is blotted out with the muzzles, or we can use maintained lead where the target remains in front of the gun at all times. The second method requires the ability to look "through" or round the gun with the other eye to maintain visual contact just as you would do with a high, driven target. With the close teal, the swing through method will work very well, providing you have the confidence to trigger the shot as the muzzles of the gun overtake the target. Failure to trigger the shot at the right time will result in head lifting and the gun will shoot high. The temptation to do this, combined with the possibility that the target is reaching the peak of its trajectory and starting to slow down, results in many teal being missed over the top.

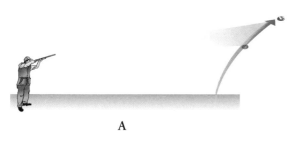

A

Both targets fall into the category of a teal target but teal A is showing less "face" and requires less lead (and gun movement) than teal B.

B

Diagram 11

So where exactly is the best place to tackle a "springer"? Often, with a presentation where two teal are thrown together as a true pair, we have four choices.

1. We can take both targets on the way up.
2. We can either take one of the targets on the way up and one at the top as it stops.
3. We can take one at the top as it stops and one on the way down.
4. We can take them both on the way down.

Which one is correct? The answer is number 2. Am I splitting hairs with this? Absolutely not. Once again, target vulnerability must be considered. So here's one of the "tricks of the trade" that you can use, you will find that it will give you extremely good consistency providing you evaluate the range correctly. Think of a springing teal as it gets to the top of its climb. For a split second, visually, it stops. Logically, any teal target must be easier to hit when it stops than it would be on the way up or down when it is moving faster. In terms of vulnerability, this must be the best place to shoot it because by shooting the target here, we have eliminated two of the variables, the angle and the speed of the target.

With a teal that stops briefly at the peak of its trajectory, many shooters will tell you to: "Shoot right at it." I always consider this to be "sloppy thinking" because the target will be either rising or falling in the area you plan to shoot it, *by the time the shot column reaches it.* The 50 yard teal may be still rising as the trigger is pulled but already falling as the shot column reaches it. This is why, on a distant teal, a reasonably accurate assessment of range is necessary.

This is what works on the "stationary" teal target. If the place where the teal stops relative to your shooting position is 20 yards away, spot shoot at the bottom edge. If the range is 30 yards, (by using the target as a visual reference), shoot 1 target widths underneath, at 40 yards, shoot 2 target widths underneath. At 50 yards, due to the now rapidly decelerating shot column, (exponential effect) it may take 4 to 5 target widths. There should be virtually no gun movement at all with this shot; this is an "ambush" or spot shooting technique. Also, the shot should be taken, in every case, as the target *visually* stops. With practice, this is easy to do. If the target has a subtle left or right sideways drift to it, it is easy to compensate for this by repositioning the gun slightly.

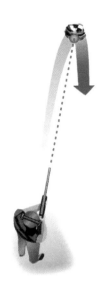

20 yard target

Spot shoot bottom edge

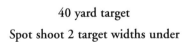

30 yard target

Spot shoot 1 target widths under

40 yard target

Spot shoot 2 target widths under

The theory here is that most sporting clay guns will pattern 60%-40%. This means that on the 20 yard target (with a standard shell of approximately 1,200 ft/second,) the shot pattern will take approximately 0.060 seconds to reach the target. The shot at the bottom edge at 20 yards *as the target stops* will center it with the pattern. With the 30 yard and 40 yards targets, the pattern will take slightly longer to get there, approximately 0.097 of a second and 0.139 respectively. So, the target will be descending slightly as the shot pattern reaches it. Once again, a spot shot of 1 and 2 target widths underneath will center these targets. Am I trying to be too precise with this? Absolutely not. Precision is very necessary for high scores.

Now I am not suggesting that you should take all springing teal like this because you must learn to break teal in three different places, on the way up, at the top and on the way down. An inexperienced shooter will often try to take both targets on the way up and this is a mistake. Let me explain why. The only way to take a teal target on the way up is by using a swing through technique or a "looking through the gun" sustained lead technique. With this type of true pair presentation, take the time to read both targets. At the point where each target peaks, how far is it? Also, one of the targets will usually be deviating more than the other from the true vertical line and this is the target to take first. On this target, the gun hold should be approximately half way between the trap and the intended break point. Gun hold too low and you will end up chasing the target with no gun control. To high and you will try to shoot the target with a dead gun. The gun hold position should be just to the side of the target's line so that it remains in view at all times. As you visually pick up the target and move smoothly onto the line, fire just as you pass it. The second target of the pair may still be rising but resist the temptation to shoot it quickly as it does so. Why? Because if you do, my guess is that you will miss over the top because you will be shooting at a decelerating target with an accelerating gun.

Instead, let this second target visually stop and shoot just underneath the target (depending on where it stops) with the lead described above. Then, move smoothly onto the second target. Doesn't this make sense? I often see shooters, faced with a report pair teal presentation, take the first teal on the way up. Why? Surely if the target is more or less stationary, as it gets to the top, it must be easier to hit?

What happens if we need to shoot one of the teal as it drops? I often see technical articles where the writer describes the battue as "the only target that accelerates as it drops". This is misleading, because several targets accelerate as they fall, the teal being one of them. With any target that accelerates as it drops, we can't use a sustained lead method, we must use pull-away. The sustained lead shot relies on the synchronization of the gun and target speeds and if the target is accelerating, then the gun must accelerate in harmony with it. All edge on teal respond well to this method but a conscious evaluation of range is important, so the visual lead as described in the transitioning target section can be applied. For example, with a 40 yard dropping teal, the visual indication would be to shoot at least 3 to 4 feet underneath.

The line also needs careful scrutiny; these accelerating teal are rarely prescribing a truly vertical line as they drop, there is usually a slight deviation to the right or left. Failure to respond to this subtle nuance will result in a miss off-line. As the teal begins its descent, insert the gun on the leading edge. Accelerate until you see the appropriate lead and trigger the shot. This must be smooth acceleration, just slightly faster than the target speed.

The best way to achieve this smooth acceleration is to bend forward from the waist, or "bow" to the target, so that the head remains firmly locked into position on the stock and you will stay in the gun. Failure to stay in the gun will mean a miss over the top, because the gun will shoot high. This "bow to the target" motion works well with all, accelerating, dropping targets.

Steeply angled teal targets

A teal, (or any other target for that matter) where the machine is angled up steeply at 45 degrees or sometimes more, can be a problem target for many of us. The reason for this is simple; because we have two legs, the human torso pivots easily on a horizontal plane, similar to a tank turret. As I have said earlier, the line is the most important thing to consider with any target and developing the line accurately on a target with a line like this is extremely difficult for most of us. A teal like this will also be edge on to your shooting position and instead of showing a lot of face; it will be difficult to break. Choke and 7 ½'s needed! As an example, think of a steeply angled left to right target. Most shooters, although they have every intention of following the difficult line will miss this target below and right because they will produce a curving gun movement on a steeply rising target. So here are two tips that often help. The first tip is a "spin-off" from a driven pheasant shooting trick. The concept is easier to apply with a side by side shotgun if we imagine a horizontal plane passing through the two barrels but once mastered , it works just as well with the over/under and semi-auto shotgun.

Two things make this method work. By dropping your LEFT shoulder and raising your RIGHT, you can make the muzzles move easier and more accurately on the line of the target. (See diagram 12.) The second thing is a slight "rotation" of the barrels towards the trap. In other words, you are canting your barrels over so that the gun is moving more parallel to the line and slicing accurately along it instead of cutting through it. By doing this we are in effect shooting a crossing target. The second way is to carefully visualize a clock face. The machine, or point where you first get a good visual contact on the target is in the center of the clock face. If the angle is really steep, the targets line may be at 1 o'clock. Less steep it may be at 2 o'clock, but by visualizing this before attempting the shot, there is a good chance that the move on the target line will be more accurate.

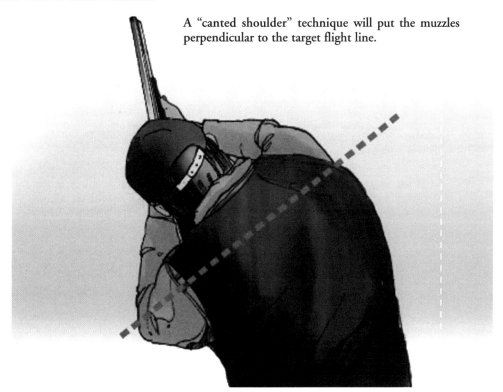

A "canted shoulder" technique will put the muzzles perpendicular to the target flight line.

Diagram 12

CHAPTER 11

Rabbits

Half the speed, half the lead!

Remember the above heading! Rabbits don't travel as fast as we think; in fact they are by far the slowest target we will encounter on the sporting clay course. But they don't appear to be, do they? Because they are low to the ground, the background of grass, bushes etc. give them the illusion that they are traveling a lot faster than they really are. Even a full crossing shot at a rabbit at 20 yards requires less than 1/2 the lead that an airborne target needs at the same distance. Why? First of all rabbits have a wide rim around the edge and a cross section would reveal that they are thicker and heavier than standard targets. They have to be, they need to be robust enough withstand breakage as they run along the ground and come into contact with stones and bits of debris, broken targets etc.

This heavier, more robust design, combined with the friction as they roll along the ground also means that they will "bleed off" energy quickly. Very quickly. All these add up to one thing; almost all shooters rush through from behind, establish too much lead and miss them in front. As they do this, the shot column kicks up a cloud of dust, the rabbit then rolls through this cloud and the optical illusion is that the miss was behind. What do we do then? Extend our lead and miss even further in front. Frustrating little beggars aren't they? Until we become more educated!

Set up and stance is important; many shooters miss targets off-line and over the top. The natural tendency with any target that is at ground level or below our feet means that without thinking, we will widen our stance slightly to provide more stability with our foot positions. A standard gunstock, has a drop at nose of approximately 1 ½ and 2 ¼ at heel, which presents the face with a fairly steep "incline" from back to front. This will mean that we may "creep" the stock and as we do this, our eye will be elevated slightly above the rib. It doesn't take much, ¼ of an inch or so at the gun end is the equivalent of a head lift, of course then the gun will shoot high as a result. (See diagram 13)

This is one of the main reasons why more and more shooters are opting for Monte Carlo style stocks; their eye will remain in the right place regardless of their head position. The address position with a rabbit should be with the muzzles well below the line of the target so that as the gun is lifted to the face, it doesn't come above the line making it necessary to drop it down again and then back up, with superfluous, wasted gun movement. In other words, the muzzles will prescribe a "check mark" instead of a smooth lift to establish the target line. The gun must be raised to the face with a "parallel action", with both hands lifting the gun in unison.

Another "trick of the trade" is to always shoot deliberately low on all rabbits. This is good advice; most sporters are designed to throw their pattern high so you can afford to aim low. Too low, and you will still break the target as the pellets ricochet off the ground.

"Creep the stock" and the pattern will go high

Always shoot low on a rabbit target.

Diagram 13

So remember, with rabbits, half the speed, half the lead is good advice. By using the unit method, once you are familiar with the units of lead that you need to give the airborne target at a similar angle and range, cut your lead in half and my guess is, you will hit far more of them. So here's something you might like to try next time you have an extra long, 50 yard rabbit target at a sporting clay tournament. You know, the sort of target that destroys most shooters. Using the unit method, you would give this target about 6 units if it was an airborne target. Cut your lead in half and give it 3 units. This takes a bit of confidence because the lead will look hopelessly inadequate, compared to an airborne target at the same range but my guess is, you'll be right in the middle of it.

Preferred method

Sustained lead is the only way. A swing through or pull away method is unadvisable in case the rabbit "hops" Any method that produces momentum in the barrels would mean that if this momentum is produced just as the rabbit hops, the gun makes a fleeting move on the wrong line and a miss is inevitable. With a sustained lead method, an adjustment can be made to correct this because the gun is in front of the target at all times.

Wind effect

A full crossing rabbit should be unaffected but beware! Any quartering in or out angle shot will develop a "curl" or hook to the right or left in the path if there is a side wind, especially as the target begins to slow and loose momentum. Diagram 3 shows this. Don't forget the line is the most important thing to consider and many shooters fail to see this subtle nuance as the shot is triggered, missing down the side of the target.

Chokes and loads

A "regular" rabbit, if there is such a thing, usually shows its full face. Even though these targets are thicker than a standard target, they are easily broken at close to moderate ranges, 20 to 30 yards for example, with fairly open chokes, skeet and improved cylinder and no 8's. Edge-on rabbits are different. Now the target will present the thick rim to the shooter and it will also be getting away fast, making it less vulnerable. In this case, a move up in choke constriction to modified and 7 ½ shot size is advisable.

CHAPTER 12

Tall Towers, Short Answers

Driven pheasant shoots originated in England in East Anglia in about 1875 and in those days teams of "beaters," would walk in an orderly fashion through the woodlands of the great sporting estates. Each beater was armed with a hazel stick, and he would thrash the undergrowth to flush the birds out, pushing them over the waiting guns. The idea was to encourage the birds to fly high and fast over the shooters to test their marksmanship. Even in those days, there were many attempts to rationalize the theories of shotgun shooting and explain the skills of the sport.

Many books were written on the subject, including one in about 1925 by the Victorian naturalist Sir Ralph Payne-Gallwey, *High Pheasants in Theory and Practice*. Later, shooting schools, notably Holland & Holland and West London, evolved so that the sportsmen and women of this era could improve their marksmanship. Which shots do you think gave these Victorian sportsmen their biggest headache? The high birds and long, crossing shots, of course and as a result, each shooting ground had its own high tower to simulate these difficult targets.

Here in the US you call high towers "duck" towers but in the UK we call them simply high towers. They originated over there to simulate "tall" pheasant shots. Today, things haven't changed much, have they? The sight of a high tower poking ominously above the tree line as we walk round a testing sporting clay course is usually enough to send shivers down our spine. Make no mistake, the high tower is a formidable opponent, the nemesis of many a good shooter. Sporting clays tournaments often are won or lost there.

I was lucky. I lived for many years in the heart of some of the best driven pheas-ant shooting in the world, the Border country in South West Scotland. It was my job to make sure that the visiting "guns" to the sporting estates of the surrounding area could manage to hit a few. This was often a daunting task for me; anyone who has been lucky enough to shoot European driven pheasants will know just how difficult the real thing is. Some of the birds would be coming over at well over 50 yards, but they appeared to be moving slowly due to the effects of perspective. A 50-yard-high hen pheasant screaming down the side of a Scottish mountain with a stiff tailwind behind it makes a clay target with a more predictable trajectory seem a lot easier by comparison.

Notice that I said *easier*, not easy, because high clay birds are anything but easy. But with a *systematic* approach, they can be beaten. High tower shots can either be driven straight toward or away from the shooter or crossing or quartering, either to the left or right. Each requires a different technique. Everything that works at closer ranges won't on the high tower because the margin for error is so exaggerated by distance. The lead requirement on a high, crossing shot deceives everyone initially and a more con-scious approach to evaluating the range is necessary. Why? Because there is an optical illusion at work here and this confuses us.

Next time you prepare to shoot a full crossing shot off a high tower make a care-ful guesstimate of the range involved. The targets from a high tower appear to move much slower than they it really are because we have absolutely no visual reference to anything as we shoot these high birds, just an empty expanse of sky. Because of this, especially on the full crossing shots, it is oh, so very easy to shoot behind them! My shooting clients are always amazed at how much daylight they need to see to break a long, fast crosser from a high tower. Instinctive shooting is easily applied to closer targets where speed assessment is easier and narrow angles call for little leads but there's a lot of fresh air around a target when it's 40 yards plus or more off the ground.

First, let's discuss the best way to tackle the straight incoming shot. Good foot positions are the key for successful tower shots. It is *impossible* to move the gun accu-rately on the same trajectory as a high crosser if your stance is wrong. With a high, incoming bird from a tower the normal stance of about five past three (right shoul-dered shooter) will be fine but if the bird is angling to the left, the stance should be opened up a bit, with the front foot pointing towards about 11 o'clock, the back foot roughly towards 2 o'clock. The target that is angled to the right may need foot positions of approximately ten past four. (See diagram14.)

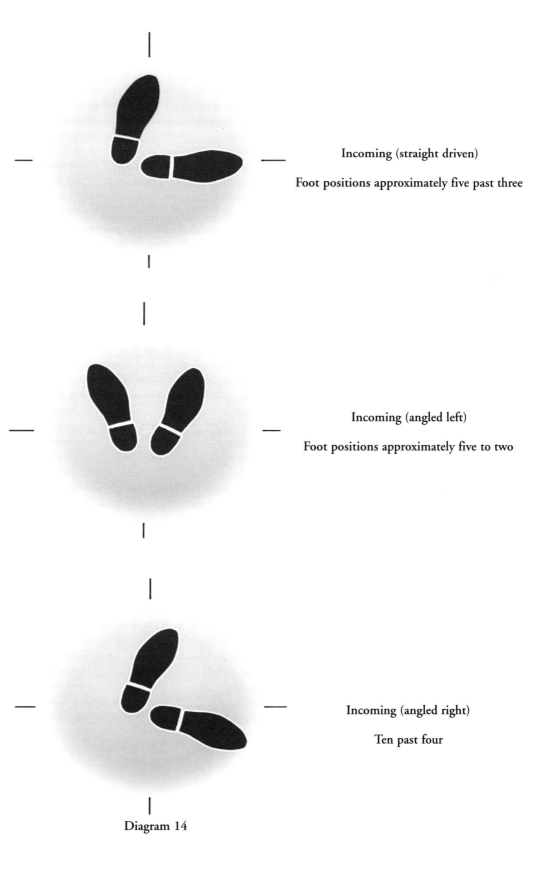

Incoming (straight driven)

Foot positions approximately five past three

Incoming (angled left)

Foot positions approximately five to two

Incoming (angled right)

Ten past four

Diagram 14

A swing through technique is the best medicine for the incoming driven targets that are coming straight towards your shooting position but these always give shooters problems. Why? Because, when we shoot any moving target, we must put the shot charge into the *anticipated* flight path, which means that a high driven bird will vanish behind the gun as we pull the trigger. (See diagram 15) Then what happens? Usually, we lift our head to look for the target, once again the gun stops and we miss behind. So how do you maintain visual contact with the target as it vanishes behind the gun? There are two ways you can do this.

You can learn to look "through" and beyond the barrels with your other eye, the left eye of a right-shouldered shooter. With practice, the correct amount of lead can be established accurately each time as the gun overtakes the target. Notice I said with *practice* because some of my clients, when they try this for the first time, don't have the faintest idea what I'm talking about and continue shooting high driven birds by guessing where the target is as they pull the trigger. With practice, this "looking through the gun" technique works extremely well on driven tower shots as well as long springing teal and some trap-type shots. For shooters with a master eye problem, the trick is to close the eye that is *not* above the rib until the line is established, then open the other eye to establish lead.

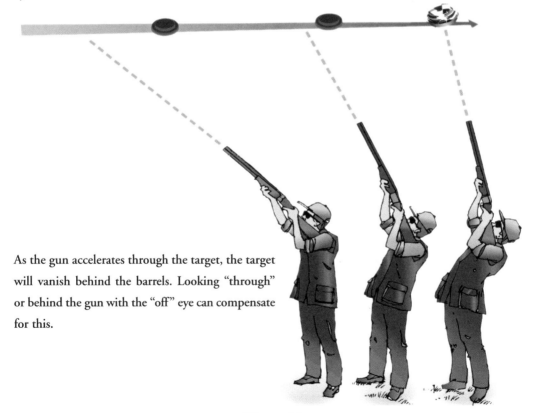

As the gun accelerates through the target, the target will vanish behind the barrels. Looking "through" or behind the gun with the "off" eye can compensate for this.

Diagram 15

Low driven targets should be taken well out in front with the weight over the leading leg. This is because the oblique angle makes them the vertical equivalent of a narrow-angle quartering target, and the lead requirement is minimal. But a true high bird of 40 yards or more is nearest to you when it is directly overhead, so, logically, this is the best place to shoot it. This means that in some cases, we must be able to move the gun past the vertical. Unfortunately this is just where most of us run out of swing, the gun stops, and we miss behind. On a high driven target, the lead requirement is considerable, so a smooth swing is essential for good results. So, how do we make sure that we can produce a smooth, accurate swing up to and beyond the vertical? When shooting incoming birds high overhead, raising the heel of the front foot transfers weight to the back foot, moving the hips forward and the upper torso back. This helps produce a smooth and assertive swing well past the vertical. On a high outgoing shot, the exact opposite is the case, your weight should be transferred to the front foot to produce a smooth, progressive gun mount in the same direction as the target. (See diagram 16)

Heel of front foot lifted slightly

A much smoother, progressive swing in the same direction as the target will be produced if you do this. Try this at home. Keep both feet firmly on the ground and move your gun to the vertical position at an imaginary target. While in this position, raise your front heel slightly. See what happens? As the heel is raised, the hips push forward, and the upper torso moves back. You should now be able to swing well past the vertical. This is a progressive, smooth movement that takes place just as the gun is coming into the shoulder, not a sudden lift with the heel. Just as with long crossing shots, most of the movement on the target line should be made with the arms.

When a high incomer is approaching right at you, with no sideways deviation to the left or right, it is difficult to swing smoothly through the target without a slight drift to the left (for right handed shooters) due to muscle tension in the extended left arm and upper body as the gun hits the shoulder. The muzzles will drag off the line and prescribing an arc and a miss down the side of the target will be the result. To compensate, move your grip on the fore end back slightly. This will also help to produce maximum swing past the vertical because there is now slightly more weight forward of the leading hand than normal, resulting in slightly more momentum in the barrels. This will help to produce a good, continuous, smooth swing as the shot is taken.

The foot positions for a wide-apart pair of driven targets, is exactly the same as the stance I recommend when shooting high driven live birds. Stand facing squarely to the tower, feet approximately shoulder width apart; any wider will restrict your movement. As the right-hand bird is taken, the *left* heel should be raised slightly to give a more flowing movement to the right, then the *right* heel is raised as the bird on the left is taken. This will ensure the shoulders remain level throughout the swing.

What about the "driven away" target? Sustained lead or pull away is the best medicine for this target. Why? Because if you attempt to swing through from behind, you will find that it takes a bit of catching. Instead of a smooth, precise movement, you will probably end up with a hurried poke and almost certainly drag the gun off-line. Every millisecond you delay pulling the trigger on this target will make it more difficult to break.

To set up yourself for this shot, put your weight onto your *back* foot and look back for the target so you will have good visual contact as soon as possible. Keep your gun fairly high, but not so far back that the barrels are out of your peripheral vision. Be prepared to move the gun on the "flash" of the target or the built-in lead allowance you have will quickly evaporate, and you will end up chasing the target. As you call for the target and begin to move the gun, allow your weight to transfer to the *front* leg. Once again, this type of target is best shot where it is most vulnerable to your gun— as near to you as possible. This is where the target is presenting its most vulnerable concave underside. Don't forget that the lead requirement will be just as much as on an incoming driven bird but this will decrease (remember the closing angle?) as the target gets further away.

Once again, the optical information you transmit to your brain will suggest that the target is moving slowly. It isn't. If its speed and distance from you are the same, then, logically, the lead must be the same. For some reason, most shooters think they can give an outgoing bird less lead than they would give a similar incoming shot. With a *pair* of driven targets off high tower, or any driven pair, for that matter, which one do you take first? Providing they are both coming toward you at the same speed, the answer for a right-shouldered shooter is the *right* one. By doing this, you will keep the gun pushed into your face as you shoot the second target. Try it the other way around, and you will probably push the gun away from your face and shoot down the side of the target.

Now let's look at high crossing targets, everybody's nemesis- but they don't need to be. This target is simply a full crosser and no different from any other, (ninety degree to your shooting position), full crossing shot. Far more crossing shots on the high tower are missed off the line than most shotgunners think. The *majority* of crossing targets on a sporting clays course or in the hunting fields require fairly horizontal gun movement but now we are faced with gun movement that is neither horizontal nor vertical but somewhere in between. This is a difficult movement for most people to make and to move an 8 ½ lb. gun *smoothly* above your head to successfully merge onto the same line of the target takes lots of practice.

The longer the gun is in your shoulder, the more conscious you become of it. Just as with the driven shot, to attempt to shoot high, crossing birds with a pre-mounted gun is a mistake. The barrel becomes a distraction because it is central to your line of vision, which makes reading the line of the target difficult. If you put the gun in your shoulder too early, the muzzles will almost certainly try to move horizontally. If the target isn't moving in a horizontal direction in relation to you, then you've got a problem. Failure to set up yourself correctly will also mean that you will run out of swing, drop a shoulder in an attempt to keep the gun moving, and "rainbow" under the line of the target. This is known as "dropping off the line." Many high crossers are missed below for this reason. (See diagram17)

Diagram 17
Beware of the rainbow!

The high crossing target is more vulnerable to the gun when it is nearest to your shooting position. Often, we can see the target come off the machine on the tower for what seems like an age before they are actually in range and vulnerable to your gun. Before the target eventually reachs the "kill zone", it is easy to become mesmerized by it and mount the gun too early. If you are not careful, this will lead to tracking, or following the target with a mounted gun. Don't do it. The secret is to use your *arms* to produce most of the movement.

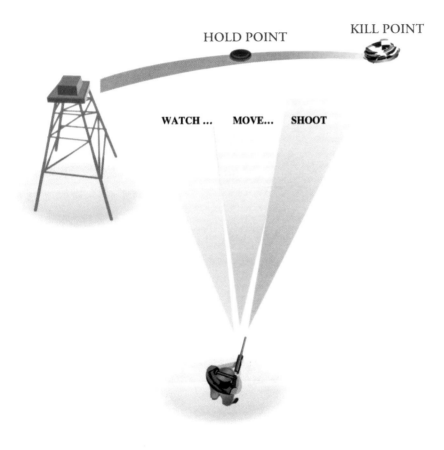

Diagram 18

A smoothly engineered movement along the line of the target (known as "developing" the line) is essential for success on this type of shot. By doing this, the shoulders will remain level as the shot is taken and ensure that there is plenty of room for a *smooth* and *assertive* swing well past the intended break point of the target. I say assertive because slowing or stopping the gun on a long, crossing shot is a sure way to invite a miss. Preferably, shoot as soon as the gun hits your shoulder to complete the mount.

The trajectory can be divided into three zones, the "watch" zone, "move" zone and the "kill" zone. (See diagram 18) The "watch" zone is the area from where you fist visually pick the target up to where your gun hold point is under the target. The second area is the "move" zone and as the target comes into this area, the gun should start moving towards the shoulder pocket. The target reaches the "kill" zone at exactly the same time that the gun mount is completed and the butt is firmly embedded in the shoulder pocket; the shot should be taken without delay as this happens. The gun should "mirror" the target speed; as I often tell students, a slow start and a quick finish.

So, assuming we get our foot positions right and can successfully move the gun on the same line as the target, the only way we can miss is in front or behind. It isn't very likely that we will miss in front, so why do most shooters miss behind? There are three main reasons. If your club has a high tower that elevates to different levels, you might like to try the following experiment. Shoot a driven target at its lowest setting, coming over you at perhaps 20 feet. Then, elevate the tower to its highest setting and do the same thing again. See how much slower the target appears to be moving? Obviously it can't be; the targets are coming off the trap arm at the same speed. That's the main reason many shooters miss high targets behind. The brain refuses to accept the ocular stimuli it receives and gives the order to fire, unfortunately, usually when the amount of forward allowance is about half of what's really needed.

To most of us, targets coming off a high tower look to be about the size of a pin head. The lead requirement is so much on some of them that as the gun pushes ahead to establish lead, the target is fast fading into our peripheral vision. So now what do we do? Look at the gun, of course, to "measure" the lead. Human eyes can't focus on two things at the same time, so guess what happens next? We stop the gun—the third reason we miss behind.

So now you're ready to take your next high, crossing shot from the tower. Decide where on the target's trajectory you will shoot it, in most cases, where it is nearest to you. Set up yourself correctly. Concentrate *mainly* on developing the line, and as soon as you see what you perceive is the correct amount of forward allowance, take the shot. The amount of perceived lead will depend on the individual and the shooting method he uses. For example, the swing-through shooter will see less lead than the pull-away or maintained-lead shooter due to the variation in the amount of gun speed. If you miss, and you *know* you were on line, the problem *must* be the amount of forward allowance you gave the target. Increase your lead. It is *almost* impossible to miss a fast, high crossing bird in front.

Finally, Good timing, perfect foot positions, and perfect balance are more important on these high crossing shots than almost any other shot. For many years, I had the pleasure of witnessing some of the best high pheasant shots in the world. The ease and unhurried elegance with which some of these guys could stroke a really high bird out of the sky was incredible. But it only comes with practice.

Preferred method

All the incoming shots can be shot using either a swing through or (by looking through the gun) a sustained lead technique. With the full crossing shots, sustained lead is best.

Chokes and loads

All incoming targets off a tower will be showing the vulnerable concave "belly" and these targets are easily broken with open chokes and 8's. For the full crossing shots, some of which may be 50-60 yards and more, 7 ½'s and tighter chokes, light and improved modified will work better.

Wind effect

If the machine is angled up slightly, wind coming from behind the shooter (as he faces he tower) will dramatically slow the target down. Too much gun speed may result in over leading the target. With a full crossing shot, any wind interference can create a problem. Often, at the split second that the correct bird/barrel is identified and the shot is triggered, the wind can push the target either up or down on the trajectory and a miss off -line is the inevitable result.

CHAPTER 13

Minis, Midis and Rockets

The midi target, especially when it is thrown in tandem with a standard target, can present a visually tricky combination. Visually, the midi is exactly the same as the standard but in a competition accurate recognition is a must. When thrown as a true pair from machines with similar spring tension, the midi will rapidly gain on the standard and overtake it. But because of the lighter weight of the midi, 74 grams as opposed to the standard targets 105 grams, this initial rapid deceleration will bleed off quickly and the target will transition rapidly. Visual discipline is of paramount importance with a combination like this and although initially visually similar, at a distance the lines of each target will be completely different. Most shooters, especially if this is a long presentation, will have too much gun speed, producing horizontal momentum with the gun barrels as they shoot the standard and what happens then? Of course the target line of the midi isn't as horizontal as they thought and you've guessed it, the shot goes over the top.

Another target that will give shooters fits, seen often in the UK but rarely seen over here is the "stealth" target, sometimes called the rocket. The stealth is similar to the rabbit, but slightly lighter at 115 grams to the rabbits 120 grams. It resembles an extra thick battue and it is used as an airborne target with a flat trajectory. Because of the weight of this target, the energy bleeds of rapidly towards the end of its flight path, once again inviting the inexperienced shooter to miss over the top

The baby of the bunch is the mini target. The mini target with a height of 21 mm also has a deeper convex surface than any other target and this light weight combined with this relatively large convex surface area makes the mini, in certain presentations, a formidable opponent. The diminutive mini, 60 mm in diameter with it's light weight a mere 35 grams, retrains very little energy and slows down quicker than any other target. It is both hard to see deceptively east to miss. Because of its small size and lack of weight the mini is deceptively fast in the early stages of its flight and this is where most of us crash and burn. When the mini is thrown from a standard machine, even one with the spring wound up, it is unusual to see them travel more than 35-40 yards. Wind the spring on the machine up too tight and these diminutive targets will break as they come off the throwing plate.

One of my favorite target presentations is a mini target coming from a machine that is positioned underneath the safety platform and going straight away from the shooter. It's a simple, going away trap-type presentation but watch what happens when the shooters take the stage! Most shooters, even a good shot with fast reactions and impeccable timing, cannot shoot any target (from the time they first visually acquire it) before it has traveled between 15-20 yards. Unless they are very careful about selecting which part on the trajectory they intend to break a mini, my guess is that a huge proportion of them will shoot over the top of it before they realize this rapid bleed off of energy is happening. On the presentation described with the wind coming into the shooters face the target will stay up forever but with the wind coming from behind the shooter, even a light gust can push the target down rapidly.

CHAPTER 14

Pair in the Air

My client, an experienced shot whom I had been coaching intermittently for almost two years, was no stranger to competitive shotgunning. When he arrived for the lesson and we walked the course, I quizzed him about which targets he would like to work on. Usually, with an experienced shooter, this initial conversation helps me to identify specific areas but on this occasion, I got the impression that there was no one target in particular that was giving him problems.

As we arrived at the first station, the menu on the plaque in front of the safety cage said five true pairs. As he entered the cage, I positioned myself next to him so that we could both get a good look at the targets.

"Let's see a pair" I said and as I hit the button, a quartering rabbit target appeared from behind a patch of scrub on our left and bounced off along a well-worn track, disappearing into a drain about thirty yards away. At exactly the same time, a quartering airborne target appeared over our right shoulders, hovering briefly before dropping quickly behind a stand of live oaks. Without hesitation, my client, with a confident smile, dropped a couple of shells into his Perazzi and called for the targets.

Bang! The fur was puffed convincingly, then Bang! The feather suffered the same fate. The Perazzi spat the spent hulls out, rattling them noisily onto the gravel at our feet. My client grinned over his shoulder at me in triumph.

"O.K. Let's see you do it again," I said, "in fact let's imagine you're in a tournament. Shoot five pairs."

Happy to oblige, my client did just that. Calling for his second pair, there was a delay as he shot the rabbit that resulted in a hurried poke at the second target. Both targets were hit but only just, the break on the bird was a bit on the "chippy" side for my liking. With his next pair, the rabbit was missed completely but the bird was hit again just! Now the wheels were coming off, big time. His last two pairs prompted a desperate change of tactics, the bird first, then the rabbit. But the damage was done and his score final for the five pairs was a very mediocre 6. As singles I doubt if he would have missed a target. So what was the problem? Concentration? Poor mechanics? At this early stage in the lesson, I wasn't sure. But I noticed that his "timing" in other words the place where he broke each pair varied considerably.

Not quite so elated now his with his very average performance, my client asked me the inevitable question;

"OK, which one should I have taken first?"

"Not sure yet, let's have another look at a pair." I replied. My answer surprised him. A full time shooting coach for many years, surely by now, I had seen enough presentations to know without a moment's hesitation, which target that should be. Not always. This particular true pair presentation wasn't easy; a narrow angle left to right and a similar narrow angle right to left. But the gun movement between the two was considerable and the presentation required thorough analysis.

But that isn't always what we do is it? You know the feeling. It's a big event, one of the biggest on the calendar and as you and your buddies arrive at the venue, tournament fever takes over. Out on the course, with giddy anticipation, you anxiously wait for your turn at a station. The true pair presentation is tricky; you're not really sure which target is the one to take first but other shooters are waiting and you don't want to look silly do you? So you have a quick look and think you've got them figured out. But you haven't and you get a final score of 7. Then, as a more experienced shooter takes the stage and you watch him shoot, you realize where you've messed up. He walks out to rejoin his buds with a high five, back-slapping 10. Then you realize that he was the guy that you casually noticed on the sidelines as you swapped jokes with your compadres. No jovial bull-whip with his buddies for this guy, he spent his time reading each pair of targets and preparing his game-plan, capitalizing on the precious moments as he waited in line before taking his turn. And then when he did get into the cage, each pair of targets was crushed in exactly the same place as the previous one. No paralysis analysis for this guy, his carefully thought out plan of attack worked on the first pair, so he stuck rigidly to it until all five pairs were broken. His gun hold position, visual collection point and rhythmic execution of each shot was identical on each pair of targets. You didn't think that sort of dedication was needed did you? If you're a fun shooter, it probably isn't. But at top level, if you really have a burning desire to win, it is. This attention to detail is what makes the difference between stepping into the winners enclosure at the end of the day, or painful relegation to the ranks of the also-ran.

Sporting clays is a game of pairs and as the game still continues to evolve over here, so do the target setting skills of the course designer. As the ante is upped, this puts a greater demand on the target reading skill of the competitor. The once simple true pair presentation can now be a complex combination of variables and present a head-scratching dilemma for many of us, especially under the stress of a competition. And believe it or not, the type of gun we use, on occasion, can influence our decision and have some impact on which target we decide to break first. The guy with the semi-auto, with his single choke choice may need to shoot his true pair the opposite way from the over and under guy with his choice of two chokes. So for all the aspiring sporting clay champions out there, here are some suggestions. Notice that I said suggestions, not rules. This is sporting clays we're playing and quite frankly, there aren't any concrete rules. But for many of us, that's the attraction to the sport isn't it? The predictable unpredictability of it all.

There are a variety of pairs that we encounter on the sporting clay course. These are the true pair, where both targets are launched simultaneously, the on-report pair where the second target is launched on the report of the gun and the following pair; usually two targets launched from the same machine. As we attempt to unravel the subtleties of each presentation there are several key questions we should be asking. Which target first? Be careful, this *isn't* always the one you see first. Where can I break it? Where do I look for the next target? Where can I break it? I often use the pool table comparison for this. When shooting pool, the top guys are masters at positioning the cue ball the optimum position for the second shot. It's the same with sporting clays. With repetitive shot gunning, the initial gun insertion point is critical and it is based entirely on the visual evaluation of *both* targets but I like to take this cue ball analogy a step further. The *second* target of a pair is the one that should dictate where the *first* target must be broken.

There are other, more complex pair combinations where a percentage of the targets of each pair can be thrown from a variable target launcher, like a wobble trap. This is perfectly legal according to the NSCA rule book but not widely accepted over here. Let's start with the simplest of the pairs, the following pair, with both targets coming from the same machine *as quickly as the machine will recycle*. On this type of pair, the trapper should always be briefed before the event to make sure that he holds his finger on the button for the two targets. If he doesn't, the competitor may get wide variety of pairs that will throw his timing off. Both the speed and trajectories of these targets should be identical but don't forget that the second target may be on a different place on its trajectory than where the first target was shot. Because of this, each target will require a different game plan to ensure success. Once the plan is made, the "timing" between the two shots should be the same. If it isn't, the plan will fall apart at the seams. I will discuss this in more detail later.

The report pair from two separate machines is the next and because of the delay with the second target (which is sent on the report of the gun) this presentation should be only marginally more difficult than the following pair. The on-report pair that consists of two widely angled targets may need a subtle step in the direction of the second target to ensure that the shoulders remain level as the shot is taken. Without this repositioning of the feet, there may be an errant move with the muzzles and drop of the true target line as the shot is taken. The true or simo pair from different machines is always the most difficult and this usually where most of us crash and burn. Report or true pairs require closer scrutiny than following pairs.

Once again, the key to shooting pairs successfully is target evaluation and as we enter the safety cage, we ask to see a pair. This allows us to pre-program our mental and physical resources that will in turn help to maximize our split-second strategy required to break each target. Only when we know *precisely* where we need to break each target, will our rhythm be the same each time, on each pair. If we make good use of this "see pair" the targets should break. If we don't, the computations of the correct target /barrel relationship will change each time and so will our gun management. Eventually the gun will be waving about all over the place and don't forget, less gun movement equals more control.

With this type of presentation, I have three main suggestions;

1. Always take the target first that you can see the least amount of time.
2. Always take the target first which has the straightest line relative to your position.
3. Try to take the first target where it has the least number of variables. It is easier to break a target before it starts to transition.

These suggestions apply to outgoing targets, incomers and also high "driven" targets. In theory, the straightest target with the least complicated lead should be easiest to shoot with and this will allow you to "buy" extra time to deal with the second. There are two exceptions to this. The first is the long the long incomer, thrown from a machine that may be 100 yards away. In this case, even though this incoming target may have the straightest line relative to your shooting position, it is often best to take the other target of the pair first because the incomer will be more vulnerable to your gun as it gets nearer to you. The second is when the target is coming over your head and going directly away from you. Once again, this target may have the straightest line but it may also take precious seconds to show itself. Once again, it *may* be advantageous to take the other target first.

Depending on the skill of the target setter, any true pair can be tricky. Think about a 40 yard, full crossing standard target coming from a machine with the spring tension wound up. To the unwary, this target visually appears to be exactly the same as a 30 yard full crossing midi with the spring backed off. But the speed of swing and lead requirement on the two targets will be completely different and visual discipline is a must. With a pair like this, set up is important. If possible, I always suggest that the toe of the leading leg is pointing towards the area where the *second* target will be broken. (See diagram 19) This is because, where possible, the *back* target should be taken first. This set up will ensure that a smooth progressive swing is maintained onto the second target. Try to do it the other way, taking the front target first and negative gun movement (albeit for a split second), will be produced as you look back to find the second target.

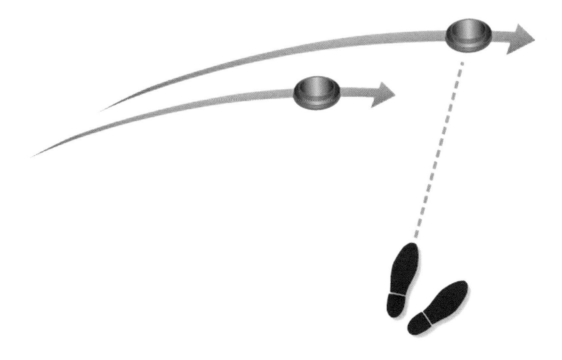

Diagram 19
The toe of the leading leg should be pointing towards
the approximate break zone of the second target

With a full crossing true pair presentation with one target on a higher trajectory than the other, always take the lower target first. (See diagram 20) Why? By taking the lower target first, the other target will remain in view. Also, a set up for the first target may mean a "rainbow" on the second target as the shoulders dip in an attempt to stay on line.

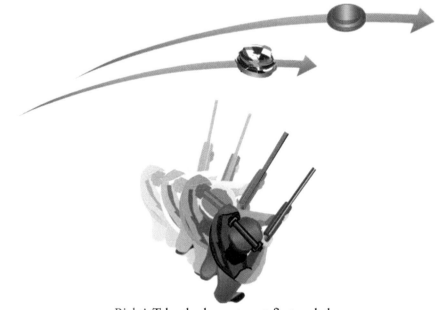

Right! Take the lower target first and the upper target remains in view at all times.

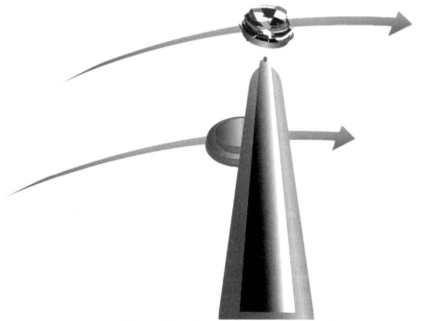

Wrong! Take the top target first and the lower target is momentarily hidden from view.

Diagram 20

With a true pair of narrow angling "quail" type presentations, the right handed shooter should take the right target first, the lefty should take the left. Why? Because if the right handed shooter takes the left target then tries to make his move to intercept the right one, chances are he will push the gun away from is face as he does this. The result? His shot may go down the side of the target. (See diagram 21)

Diagram 21

This can also be the case with a pair of dropping targets. If the lower target is shot first, then the barrels must move in an upward direction to intercept the higher target. Negative gun movement will be produced. In other words, the gun is moving up but the target is moving down. A shot over the top may be the result. (See diagram 22)

Rhythm as we shoot pairs is important. Good rhythm helps to promote unhurried elegance as the shots are triggered and it also reduces any superfluous, unnecessary movement. It's known as economy of movement and rhythm in the shot and this is particularly important as we shoot pairs. Don't forget the three "R's": Rushing Ruins Rhythm. Let me explain what I mean by this.

Diagram 22

Many years ago, I read a book that was written by a professional tennis coach. I'm afraid that name of the author escapes me but one part of the book was dedicated to exactly this. This particular coach found that sometimes, especially with young newcomers to the game of tennis, this rhythm wasn't always readily apparent in the early learning stages. This is always the case any hand eye coordination sport when and intermediary is involved, be it a tennis racquet, baseball bat or shotgun. What the tennis coach found was that most of his students could return the ball over the net far easier by the application of a simple rhythmic exercise. He would get his students to recite BALL (as they visually acquired the ball) BOUNCE (as the ball hit the ground in front of the student) and HIT as the racquet came into play to return the ball. In other words, they returned the ball to a rhythm of three beats. The success rate of the students increased dramatically, there was no superfluous wasted movement of the racquet and they were eventually returning the ball over the net with much greater consistency.

Exactly the same thing can work for us with sporting clay presentations. If possible, with a following pair, make a mental note of your gun hold point as you call for the first target. Then, take the gun out of your shoulder after shooting the first target and return to your original hold point as you visually pick up the second target. If you don't do this, any variation with the hold point will change your timing as you attempt to shoot the second target. A hold point that is too far back will mean that the target may then overtake the muzzles, resulting in a hurried chase after the target and a big change in the speed of swing. What happens then? As the "tempo" between the shots varies, your consistency goes out of the window. With many report and true pairs this dropping the gun out of the shoulder momentarily can also be an advantage. Think of a true pair presentation where the first target is a trap type target requiring little gun movement, followed by a long, slow incomer. Visual contact on the second target will be much better, if the distraction of the barrels is reduced by dropping the gun out of the shoulder pocket momentarily. But the rhythmic timing on each pair must be impeccable.

As an example of this, next time you are at a tournament, watch and listen to one of the better competitors as he shoots his targets. As he calls pull, count the "rhythm" he applies to each target on each pair. Let's say for example, his first target is a trap type presentation, (just described) followed by the incomer that appears from 80 yards away. The pair may be shot to a five beat rhythm, something like "Pull" "bang" (as he shoots the trap target, the gun now comes out of the shoulder pocket) then three, four (remount) "bang" as he shoots the incomer. It's hard to describe this on paper but I'm sure you get the idea. Of course the "tempo" will change with the variations of each pair of each presentation but my guess is that on each pair his rhythm will be identical. Of course it has to be if he is to be consistent. If it isn't, then each target will be shot in a slightly different place on its trajectory and because of this, his sight picture will change slightly as a result.

Finally, the skilled target setter must walk a fine line between what will be acceptable and a "fair pair in the air" and what is impossible. Widely angled true pairs that do not allow for an adjustment of foot position are a mistake in my book. These are "trick" shots and they have no place in a tournament. Left-handed shooters should also be given special consideration. A acceptable pair presentation for a righty may be have the lefty attempting gyrations that would make a Turkish belly dancer envious as he tries to execute his second shot. Recently, I was coaching a client who was a lefty. For the right handed shot, the true pair presentation we were working on was easy; a right to left chandelle that dropped behind a line of mesquite trees, followed by a right to left quartering incomer. The machine for the incomer was positioned about 60 yards away and the target came in rapidly and then vanished round the side of the safety cage. The incomer could have been taken first, but there would still be an uncoordinated "poke" at the now rapidly falling chondel by shooting the presentation in this way. There was no choice, the chondel was the target to take first. This particular presentation didn't cause any problems for a right handed shooter who could position himself to the right of the cage but of course as a left shouldered shooter attempted the same strategy, he ran out of swing because of the left hand vertical on the safety cage. On that occasion, that particular presentation was at a small, non-competitive corporate event. But if the same presentation had been at a tournament, I suspect that the organizers would have had very red faces! The answer? Experienced target setters should learn to mount their guns in the left shoulder so they can then go through the motions of shooting each presentation as a lefty.

CHAPTER 15

Some Examples

So now, let's say you've read this book and you are ready to try this system out in real shooting situations. My advice would be to read the book again. There is a lot of technical information in here to inwardly digest. A thorough understanding of how and (more importantly) why this system works is necessary if you are to become a better shot. To help you to start applying a logical approach to each presentation, let's look at two examples.

Example 1

Report pair, a narrow angle rabbit and a 20 yard full crossing midi. The rabbit machine is just to the left of the safety cage and the target is going from left to right at approximately 30 degrees to your shooting position. In the area you intend to shoot the target, it is approximately 20 yards away. If this was an airborne target, the lead requirement would be 2 units. But it's a rabbit target, remember, half the speed, half the lead so a 1 unit of lead will work on this target. The other target is at approximately 90 degrees to your shooting position. *Make a careful evaluation of the range.* At approximately 20 yards, this target will need a 4 unit lead.

Let's say now we have the same pair of targets but now the presentation is a true pair. Take the straightest target first which is the rabbit with a 1 unit lead. The crossing midi will now be shot later on its trajectory and no longer a full crossing shot. Now the target (in the area you intend to shoot it) will be at approximately 30 yards away and approximately 50-60 degrees to your shooting position. In this position, the target will fall into the category of a wide angle shot, so the perceived lead will be less, perhaps 2-3 units. The target is also slowing down and dropping slightly (remember diagram 9) so a "rectangle" shot will work, perhaps two feet under. The same target further along this trajectory (at about 40 yards or so) would now need a "box" shot of approximately a 3 foot square box.

Example 2

Report pair. Straight away mini, wide angle angle chondel. The mini machine is underneath a shooting platform and the target is going directly away with almost zero angular lead. The chondel machine is about 20 yards to the left of the safety cage and the target is going out at approximately 45 degrees. The mini appears to be fast and it is, initially. But careful scrutiny will reveal that *in the area you intend to shoot it*, (which is about 25-30 yards from the shooting platform) energy is already bleeding off big time and the target is beginning to transition. Most shooters will fail to notice this and shoot over the top. Now what about the chondel? This target, in the area you intend to shoot it would be classified as a wide angle target and a three unit lead should break it. Gun hold position will be the critical factor here. If the target is to be intercepted on the early part of its trajectory as it is still rising, the gun hold should be half way between where it comes into hard focus and the intended break point. A gun hold that is too close to the trap will result in too much gun movement. Momentum in the barrels may carry the gun over the top of the target as it reaches the peak of its parabolic arc. Remember your "rhythm" on this target.

If we now shoot the same pair as a true pair, the mini must obviously be taken first because it is the straightest target. The chondel will now be further out and the angle relative to your shooting position will now be reduced (closing angle). A two unit lead should break this target now but you will now need to shoot below it because the target is well past the transitional phase. If, in the area you shoot the chondel it is approximately 40 yards away, it will need a two unit lead and approximately 3-4 feet underneath for successful interception.

So there we have it, a logical approach to reading targets. Initially, applying this system will be confusing at times but persevere. It does work and, like everything it gets easier with practice.